# SOMERSAULT

## THE INGLY WRITERS

*Laura Bottaro Costner*

*Janet Gastil*

*Eddy Heubach*

*Barb Huntington*

*Kristine Limont*

*Millie McCoo*

*Philip Shafer*

*Karen Simons*

*Kary Lynn Vail*

*Suzanne Williford*

# Somersault

## An INGLY Writers

## Prose & Poetry Anthology

## Volume 1

Compiled and Edited

By

**Laura Bottaro Costner**

**INGLY Publications**

San Diego

# INGLY Publications

Pathos, Poignancy, Pungent Slap-stick Comedy. London, Wall Street, Concert Halls; Tibet, India, Zambia, and French-Canadian Fishing Yawls. Exclusive Boarding School for Juniors, Shabby Nursing Home for Seniors. Childhood Adventures, Traumas, and Memories of Mama.

## INGLY PUBLICATIONS

### San Diego

*To the memory of*
*Suzanne Williford*
*who captivated us with her*
*stories of the Deep South*

# CONTENTS

Preface

We Write,

To Taste Life Twice,

In the Moment and,

In Retrospect.

Anais Nin

# Preface

The INGLY Writers formed after meeting in a Memoir writing class at San Diego State University in 2013. The name grew out of a lengthy discussion on the overuse of gerunds and adverbs. We decided to call the group the INGLY Writers in honor of a vow to use –ing and –ly less frequently.

Our approach to the craft differs greatly. What we have in common is a desire to write stories that live in each of us as clearly as we see them in our minds. Some of the authors have published, some for the first time here.

The selection of poems and short stories cover a wide range of topics set in various time frames. Some are nostalgic, sad, or touching; others uplifting, funny, or revealing. This diverse group of writers will take you back to childhood challenges, immerse you in exotic cultures, and engage you in the many facets of everyday life. As you journey through the pages, we hope the works inspire, ignite your imagination, or just make you smile.

Our thanks and appreciation to Kathi Diamant, for her instruction in storytelling and to the Osher Lifelong Learning Institute at San Diego State for programs that bring together people who thrive on the exchange of ideas. A special thanks to Philip Shafer who served as an advisor and thanks also to members of INGLY Writers who have come and gone over the years for sharing their writings and, especially, John Castell who inspired everyone with his excellent writing skills and thoughtful critiques.

Laura Bottaro Costner

## THE MILK MAIDS
### Millie McCoo

Do you think you're big enough to go to the grocery store on your own?" my mother asked. She was standing in the doorway to the den, where my sister Marilyn and I were playing Go Fish on the rug. It was the summer of 1953. Marilyn was almost 10 and I was eight years old. We leaped up from our card game and followed our mother into the kitchen. Would she really let us go to the store by ourselves? My sister tried to appear cool, but I knew she was excited, too.

My mother was a physician and shared a family practice with my father. During the weekends, however, when Mrs. Crawford, our caretaker, was off, my mother focused on running the household while my father saw patients on his own. She did her paperwork on the kitchen table where we saw the familiar red and white carton of Ralph's milk. "I forgot, we're almost out of milk," she said. "I want you two to go to Ralph's and buy some. Can you do that for me?"

We couldn't restrain ourselves and jumped up and down in our white socks. "Yes, yes!" we squealed.

1

"Listen, now. Pay attention." We stood still, erased our smiles and put on serious faces.

"Be sure to buy Ralph's brand."

"We know, we know," my sister said.

"Now, I want four cartons," my mother continued, "The half-gallon size, okay?" She wrote "four half-gallon cartons" on a slip of paper, creased it in half, added a $10 bill and folded it once again before placing it into the hip pocket of Marilyn's shorts. "Don't lose it," she said and patted the pocket.

"I won't," Marilyn promised.

"Now remember to bring back the change. No buying candy or sodas or anything. Understood?"

"Yes, Mommy," we said in chorus as we ran to put on our shoes. The store was six blocks from our house, a skip, hop, jump and run down the sunlit, palm tree-lined streets of our residential neighborhood for three blocks; then onto Washington Boulevard in the commercial section of Los Angeles known as the Crenshaw Area.

The sun warmed me, but not as much as the thought that I had earned my mother's trust to run an errand, even if it wasn't all by myself. To me, my mother was perfect; she could do everything: doctor people, sew, cook, garden, turn herself into a stunning beauty when she dressed up to go out at night with my father. Because she was so perfect, we felt she expected the same of us.

We passed through the double glass doors of Ralph's grocery and headed toward the dairy section in the back. We found the bright red and white Ralph cartons.

"How much did she say to get?" I asked Marilyn.

"Four," she said, and then reached into her shorts pocket, pulled out the paper, carefully pushing the 10-dollar bill back in. "It says four and one-half gallons."

We scanned the shelves, but could only see smaller cartons, not the half-gallon size we were used to. We found a store clerk who told us they only had quarts left. "What should we do?" I asked Marilyn. "Maybe we should call Mommy."

"Why? Let's just get four and a half gallons like she asked. We can figure out how many cartons to get."

"Okay," I agreed.

"I don't have a pencil. Do you?" she asked.

A slender man in a gray business suit overheard us as he passed by. "Can I help you girls?"

We hesitated. Then my sister said, "Do you have a pencil?"
"Nope, but I have a pen," he said with a smile. He pulled one out of his pocket and reached toward the paper. "Here, let me help."

"We can do it," my sister said. She found a flat glass shelf on which she put the paper. Several adults passing by slowed down to watch my sister and me, shoulder to shoulder, our bodies bent over the shelf, our heads together, as we talked in low whispers. Four quarts to a gallon, right? No, there's eight . . . Wait, wait. That's pints. We're getting quarts ... so four, like I said. Now, do we multiply or divide?

With our basic arithmetic, my sister and I calculated how many quarts equaled 4 ½ gallons. Eighteen cartons. We calculated again, then again to make sure. Yep, 18!

3

I thought, how can mommy expect us to carry so many cartons? I visualized brown paper bags stacked up in our arms and blocking our eyes.

After loading the grocery cart, we pushed toward the checkout as the wheels squealed, on the way returning the pen to the gentleman who'd loaned it to us. In the checkout line, I tried to ignore the attention other shoppers focused on us and our load. I pinched my shoulders back to look taller. We were going to make Mommy proud.

As she rang up the cartons, the checker told the bag boy to get an empty produce box, rather than using bags. She took the money from Marilyn and said, "A box will be easier for you both to carry."

My sister took the change and the receipt and jammed them into her pocket. She and I struggled to get our hands under the edges of the box. After we lifted it, I found I would be walking backward while Marilyn would move forward. We knew this wouldn't work, so we plopped the box back on the counter and turned to the side. Then we picked it up and slowly crab-walked out of the store to comments of "Good luck" and "Be careful" coming at us from all directions.

As we struggled out, shoppers who entered stepped aside. I smashed the top of my right toes as we squeezed sideways through the narrow swinging doors. "Ouch!"

We slowed down when we reached the sidewalk of Washington Blvd. and began our trek toward 10th Avenue. As we shuffled along I avoided the cracks on the ground, so I wouldn't trip or bring on bad luck. My sister sped up and I stumbled, then fell onto my knees, skinning them both, but I kept the box upright.

Two women who looked about our mother's age, wearing low heels and flowery dresses, approached and asked if we were okay. My sister said we were fine, thank you. They watched us as we struggled past them.

When we came to the first corner, we stopped and waited for the light to turn green. My sister stepped down first and the edge of the box on my side slipped. I gasped. One of the cartons dropped out onto the street.

"Here, let me help you." A man in a beige mechanic's coverall bent down, picked up the carton and placed it into the box. "Be careful now. Maybe you need a ride."

Marilyn told him we were okay walking. When we stepped up on the opposite sidewalk, my sister growled, "Be more careful!"

I kept my eyes glued to the sidewalk. I could hear the traffic and see the shoes of people walking back and forth past us. A fire engine screamed from behind me and as tempted as I was, I didn't look up as it passed. The sun grew stronger and I could feel the sweat trickling down from my armpits.

Time crawled along with us down the boulevard. When would we reach our quiet, shady street? On the next corner, we saw a pay phone. Marilyn told me to stop, and we lowered the box to the ground. "I'm going to call home," she said. I felt like a failure, but I was so relieved.

Marilyn dropped in a dime and dialed. As we waited for my mother to answer the phone, I felt like I would throw up. I dreaded the disappointment I was sure I would see on my mother's face. My identity was wrapped up in her approval.

While my grades in school weren't outstanding, my mother proudly shared my love of words with all her friends. I won all the spelling bees and scored highest in my class in reading.

5

When it came to practical matters, like running errands, she usually relied on our oldest sister, Glenda. This was our time to show how grown up we were. I felt I had failed. I couldn't blame it all on Marilyn.

"Mommy," I heard my sister say, finally, "We need you to come pick us up."
"Because, we can't carry the box all the way. We're tired."
"Because there would be too many bags to carry so we had to get a box."
"No, there's lots more. There's eighteen of them."

My sister listened for a long time. Then she hung up and in a barely audible voice said, "She's coming."

When Mommy arrived in the green Ford station wagon, her face was scrunched up in a scowl. She opened the rear door on the curb side and watched us struggle into the middle seat with our load. She looked at the box, shaking her head. "What am I going to do with 18 cartons of milk?" We knew she wasn't talking to us.

As she pulled away from the curb, she said, "Now, tell me about your shopping trip."

Marilyn and I went into a high-pitched duet. "They didn't have. . ."

"One at a time," our mother said.

Marilyn rushed into the short silence. "They didn't have big cartons. They only had quart cartons. So, we had to get 18 cartons to equal four and a half gallons."

"But…" my mother started. "Four and a half gallons? I wanted four half-gallon cartons, the big ones. That's two gallons, total. That's all we needed."

Marilyn pulled out the slip of paper from her pocket, looked at it, then flinched.

A silence followed that made me squirm in my seat. I could see my mother's eyes reflected in the rearview mirror and I noticed tears. The back of her shoulders began to bob up and down. Uh-oh. I felt so ashamed. Look at what we'd done.

Tears welled up in my eyes. No, no, no! I thought to myself. I can't cry. I was the cry baby of the family: I cried at movies, I cried if I saw an injured animal, I cried at the sight of someone else crying, even if I didn't know them. The thought of disappointing my mother risked opening the floodgates. But, if any tear spilled over my bottom eyelid and slid down my cheek, Marilyn would blab about it to everyone. I fought to hold it in. It wasn't until she parked the car in the driveway that I realized my mother wasn't crying.

"What till I tell ya fatha!" she said, her Jersey accent cutting the "r's" off the ends of her words.

Marilyn and I looked at each other. This was a good sign. You never heard my mother's Jersey accent unless she was in a good mood. So, we weren't in trouble, after all. And no scolding. My body relaxed and the knot in my stomach dissolved.

"Well," Mommy said between chuckles, "You'll know better next time."

She said next time. I took a quick swipe at my cheek to hide any evidence of a tear.

## SECRET ADVENTURES
### Suzanne Williford

When I was old enough to walk up steps, I became old enough to go on secret adventures with my maid, Emma. Emma was selected by my parents to care for me primarily because she loved me so much and secondly for her ability to clean a house. She looked after me from my second birthday on. I loved her like I did my own mama.

Our adventures usually occurred after an early lunch and my midday nap. Emma dressed me in my white, pink or yellow dotted Swiss pinafore, matching ruffled panties and socks, and my freshly polished gleaming white leather high-top shoes before heading out. My clothes were just right for those humid and still summer afternoons in the South.

Emma and I would walk hand in hand about a half block to the city bus stop to wait for our bus. When it arrived, I was expected to quickly climb the three or four steps leading to the seating area. Those steps were so high. It was all I could do to stretch my little legs up to board the bus. Emma made me sit in the front of the bus while she continued all the way to the back. She would put me up on the seat right behind the driver where I could see her and she could easily see me. Sometimes I would cry because I was scared sitting in the midst of all those strangers. Eventually, Emma would make her way up the aisle and extend her hand to me, signaling it was time to get off the bus. The trip lasted only five or ten minutes, but it seemed like an eternity.

The fun part began when we reached the ice house. In the afternoon, the 'ice men' were returning from their morning delivery rounds. Everyone was in a good mood, laughing and joking and sitting around cooling off with an ice cold Coca-Cola. All of these men were so nice to me. And they always had a lollipop or piece of hard candy to share. It tasted so good after my long bus ride. It was so different from the sweets I tasted at home. While I played, sang and ate candy with the ice men, Emma was meeting up with her own 'special friend'.

I was never quite ready to leave and go back home, but Emma would hurriedly whisk me away. We then repeated our bus journey in reverse. We always arrived back home before my parents returned from their work. Emma told me to keep our travels secret or we wouldn't be able to go to the ice house anymore. I never disclosed any of this to them.

# VARANASI: A COLLISION WITH ANTIQUITY
## Laura Bottaro Costner

wo white poles held up the bold sign over a busy street food stand. The sign read '5 Star Restaurant' in big red letters. Cement drums contained fires that kept the woks hot, while a banner draped around the front of the stand advertised breakfast, lunch and dinner. By all accounts, it was a far cry from other five star Indian restaurants, but marketing is everything even on an ancient street leading down to the Ganges in Varanasi, India's holiest city. For the Americans on a tour of Northern India, the sign was comic relief in an otherwise intense and, at times, immensely soulful afternoon.

The jitney bus transported Kerry and her husband, Jake, along with the rest of the tour group from their hotel to some of the most crowded streets in all the world. Twenty minutes later it came to an abrupt stop aside an alley lined on both sides with bicycle rickshaws. Kerry's first thought was, 'At last, we are about to meld into India.' Her second was 'Oh my God the tour guide is handing out masks because, what? the fumes, the dust, hopefully, not the people?' Before she could give voice to her thoughts they were hurried off the bus and into the waiting rickshaws amidst honking horns and beeping motor

11

scooters orchestrated by impatient drivers trying to get around the bus.

When the bicyclist hopped on, Kerry and Jake looked at each other in disbelief. "He must be 60 years old and weigh 110 pounds," blurted Kerry. Jake, who recalled Kerry's pledge to only ride in motorized rickshaws, could offer a mere sympathetic, "I know but it's not like we have a lot of choices." The rickshaw moved forward before he finished his words of consolation. One by one they entered the already packed road and their Ganges adventure was underway. Kerry scanned the group to see if anyone had put on the masks. No one had. 'Good' she thought.

Their slow progress gave them plenty of time to survey their surroundings. Stand after stand offered all kinds of street food, shops and stalls were full of bright colored bolts of material and racks of saris and shirts in yellow, red, and aqua blue lined both sides of the road. Orange, the color for festivals, was everywhere. Interspersed among the stalls were temples of all sizes. Some were a simple pillar with flowers, others a building or just a façade. A steady stream of pilgrims, tourists and locals walked up and down both sides of the road with one eye on the traffic.

They began to absorb their surroundings and blend in with the mayhem. But then it was time to turn left. The driver maneuvered through a roundabout which consisted of a small pillar in the center of the intersection. Five streets emptied into the space they occupied; they could reach out and touch people on either side of the rickshaw. As they inched their way around the circle, the sounds of horns and engines went up countless decibels. They looked at their driver and then each other. Kerry began to laugh. "This is better than an old E-ride at D-

land. He doesn't feel vulnerable, let's pretend we're not."
After what seemed like an eternity, they arrived at the road to
the river. A couple of short blocks later the rickshaws pulled
into another alley and they disembarked to walk the rest of the
way on the pedestrian-only stretch of the road.

A sea of human voices replaced the sound of honking horns.
Drums and cymbals grew louder as the crowds moved toward
the river. Some stopped at stalls along the way. One could
hear, "Oh sorry" and "Nameste" over and over as people
bumped into each other.They hadn't even reached the ceremo-
nies but Kerry started to feel drawn into the oneness that
Hindus believe unites all living things, the belief that all dif-
ferences are of degree and not kind. Kerry, a true product of
western philosophy and its emphasis on the individual, had a
limited feel for community. To her, groups form, dissolve and
reform depending on the issues, just so many temporary alli-
ances. Regardless of the books she had read and classes she
had taken in Eastern philosophy and Indian culture, she never
got past an intellectual understanding of 'oneness'—even in
yoga classes. But in Varanasi one became India. Kerry could
feel herself becoming at one with that long unchanging 5000
year old culture. She felt connected to every person in the
crowd and could barely get the words out, "This is why I came
to India." Jake took one look at her watery eyes and knew a
smile was better than words.

A block later they caught up with a few of their fellow travel-
ers who pointed to the '5 Star Restaurant' sign. The
proprietor's sense of humor gave everyone a good laugh. That
and the aromas of ginger and cardamom coming from the
woks brought Kerry back to earth. Jake snapped a picture.
The music grew ever louder so they knew the water was close

but just ahead the procession slowed down.   The crowd seemed to split as if to go around something.  Eventually they reached the detour only to find a well-fed white cow lounging on the ground.  Honored for its gentle nature and contributions of food, labor and fuel, the sacred animal sat in a circle of free space about 10 feet wide.  In a crowd of thousands, that was real reverence.  They passed by the 'deity' and were soon distracted by hustlers, like the person who reached out to shake Jake's hand, gave it a 5-second massage then turned his palm upward in hope of rupees.   There were children selling flowers.  There were some souls so at peace in the chaos they were able to sleep against anything that didn't move.  And there were scantily clad Yogis.

When the water was in sight, the scene exploded. To the right a stage with seven young priests dressed in white chanted with bells and cymbals.  Drums beat out a rhythm.  The sounds of the festival and the smell of burning sandalwood filled the air. It was magical. White lights and torches grew brighter as dusk set in. The backdrop was a huge temple, one of many temples and palaces along the Ganges.   All of these festivities took place at the Dasaswamedh Ghat, one of eighty-seven ghats, or sets of stone steps, that led down to the water.   The guide pulled the group together which was no small feat in the carnival atmosphere that many in the group would have been satisfied to participate in the rest of the night.  His job was to get everyone on one of the boats at the bottom of the steps. They were there to travel up the river to Manikarnika Ghat, the funeral ghat where the majority of bodies are cremated.

Hundreds of people boarding different colored row boats at the same time took some quick gymnastics. A one-two half jump was called for followed by a rebalancing act as the boats banged into each other and bounced around in the water. At last they moved out into Mother Ganga and one man in each boat rowed the onlookers along the ghats. As it grew darker, the torches and white lights of the Dasaswamedh Ghat receded in the background but not the drums.

"Duck" the Texan who was seated in the front of the boat hollered. He had such a commanding voice that everyone ducked. People seated in the back didn't know what they ducked to avoid until a swarm of mosquitos buzzed by their heads. Laughter broke out and the group experienced the true advantage and often underrated benefit of a tour, the ability to laugh together. Oneness felt good as it always does when groups form but it didn't spill over to include the people in all the other boats. Unlike walking down the road in the middle of a crowd, the boats separated people and Kerry could read the 'us vs. them' looks on most of her fellow countrymen. This was so despite the fact that the group was well informed with only a few who had little real knowledge of India and her history. Kerry and Jake had chosen this particular tour company because their primary source of travelers was alumni organizations and university foundations. Some were more than good travel companions. A high school English teacher from Oregon jotted observations in her journal all throughout the trip. Once home, she wrote and emailed a poem 'India 2015: Color Culture Contrasts Cuisine.' Some exchanged books. A retired art teacher from Minnesota, transferred images from photos onto fabrics and made a collage which she photographed and also emailed to everyone. In this way the unity within the boat extended beyond the trip.

Soon it was completely dark and the only fires to be seen were the funeral fires. The guide reiterated that there were to be no

pictures when they got up close to the ghat. "Up close" came
to have many interpretations. Cameras clicked away from the
first sighting to distances close enough to count the fires but
not close enough to see the mourners. Generally a private af-
fair, one can attend, some might say 'intrude on', this sacred
ceremony for a price.    To Hindus cremation on the Ganges
frees the soul from the cycle of death and rebirth. The fires
burned brilliantly on the dark hillside and were a visual feast,
but the sacredness of the funerals appeared to be lost on the
group, either because cremation has become commonplace in
American culture or because the distance between the boat and
the ceremony was too great to feel a connection.

After twenty minutes at the site, most were glad to be headed
back to the music and chanting.  When they got back to the
dock, they were literally pulled off the boat along with hun-
dreds of pilgrims whose boats arrived at the same time.  No
one seemed to mind the bedlam, they were consumed by the
festival atmosphere.  Back on land, they had only to retrace
their steps to the waiting rickshaws that would take them to
the bus.

All the drivers knew their way to the bus but that didn't mean
they took the same routes or short cuts.  As Kerry and Jake's
driver turned onto a dark side street with almost no one in
sight, they actually began to miss the sound of honking horns.
They couldn't see any of their group.  Kerry wasn't feeling
'oneness' at that moment. They went through an intersection
with only a handful of scooters and rickshaws and turned into
another dark and empty street. "I don't like this," Kerry whis-
pered.  Jake ever calm tried to assure her, "Relax, he knows
where he is going."   A few minutes later she spotted a rick-
shaw way down the road.  She couldn't quite make them out

but thought it might be the older couple from New York. "They look short and have grey hair." Jake gave his usual reply when he didn't know something, "Could be." Kerry kept straining to identify them when all of a sudden the rickshaw stopped. They thought they would have to get out and find their way back to the hotel. Kerry blurted the obvious, "We have no maps nor any idea of where we are." Jake tapped the driver on the shoulder, "Are you waiting for someone?" No answer. Kerry and Jake looked around and waited. And waited. About the time Jake tapped the driver a second time, Kerry turned to see if any of their group was coming up behind them. That's when she spotted the couple from Texas; the only other people from the group they saw before reaching the alley where they left the rickshaws and boarded the bus back to the hotel.

The next morning the group was up at five to get down to the river by daybreak for more sacred ceremonies. Minimal traffic allowed them to ride the bus almost all the way to the ghats. No rickshaws. There are six special bathing days on which thousands wade into Mother Ganga to wash away their sins. Fortunately that was not one of them. It was a peaceful morning. Intermittent clouds played hide and seek with the sun which had just begun to come up behind the hills on the other side of the river.

They boarded a boat and once out on the water they were each given a small foil dish containing 1 red and 3 orange chrysanthemums that encircled a candle. Once the candle was lit they were told to make a wish and float it in the water to honor Mother Ganga. Tourists engaging in aarti, the prayerful ritual to honor a deity, felt to Kerry more like an empty gesture than sacred worship which was probably why hers sank almost

17

immediately.   This freed her up to observe others as they
watched their candles float away.  Some were also unmoved,
others somewhat solemn still others were primarily concerned
with candles going out.

When all the offering candles and flowers had floated away,
the boat took the group along the ghats where people do their
laundry and those where people bathe themselves.   Pilgrims
scrimp and save to travel to Varanasi to bathe in the Ganges.
No confessions, no penance, just a soak in Mother Ganga.
The guide books advised against bathing in India's rivers or
oceans, citing foreigners' inadequate immune system for the
types of microorganisms in the water.   That made sense espe-
cially to the doctors in the group but what most people feared
was floating body parts.   When the funerals are complete the
ashes are dumped in the River.  Unfortunately with hundreds
of cremations per day, the burning of the bodies is not always
'complete'. A good humored man from Missouri, spoke for all
when he quipped, "No splashing?  No worries."

As Kerry and Jake, along with a few others, went down a side
street on the way back to the bus, they happened upon a corpse
laying on the ledge of a temple.   The body was wrapped in
pinkish-red colors.   Everyone stopped, stood still and stared.
The anthropologist from Arizona pointed out that funerals are
sold as a kit and that appeared to be the case. There were bun-
dles of straw and two stacks of fire wood.   A red and blue
striped blanket covered the top of the wood and a ladder-like
stretcher made of tree branches lay across one of the piles.
The Untouchables, the only people allowed to conduct crema-
tions, would use the stretcher to transport the body to the
funeral ghat.    Jake took a picture.   Someone said a quiet
"Nameste" and like a chorus, the group repeated "Nameste."

Kerry was starstruck. She couldn't take her eyes off the thin colorfully wrapped body. Here was a corpse on the ledge of a building awaiting the evening funeral like one would wait for a bus. Not a symbol, not an image, but death itself right there on a ledge where people passed by as they went about their business. Kerry felt an unmistakable peacefulness wash over her. She turned to Jake and whispered, "If only I can rekindle this calm state of mind when death comes knocking at my door."

The stunned group drifted away from their head-on collision with the ancient world, the backdrop of modern India. They exchanged whatever knowledge they had of Hindu beliefs about life and death. When their expertise showed its limitations, the conversation moved on to the philosophy of oneness. Someone quoted Thoreau who claimed to have "felt illuminated by some unearthly and unknown light" whenever he read India's sacred documents. More than all the ancient ruins and medieval palaces they had visited, it was the festival the previous night and the ready acceptance of the life cycle as evidenced by the waiting corpse that left them, if not illuminated, completely fulfilled. India does not disappoint those who want to experience the ancient world in the 21st century.

## BUTTERFLY OF BELIEF
### Barb Huntington

When I was a child, the butterfly of belief
Brushed a filmy wing across my forehead
"Chase me, chase me."
Through churchyards and headstones
I reached out and grasped
Soft wings against my palm
I held, released her
Slept

In my youth, she hid behind napalm clouds of war
Fluttered above a guitar in songs of peace and equality
Was forgotten in the headiness of first love
Lit briefly in the comfort of a second
Not knowing if I really held her
Pretended her presence
For my children

In middle age, children gone to chase their own butterflies,
No infinite sky, no fluttering form, a shadowed memory
In the dark cramped rooms of death

Parents, friends, my dying love
His mind and body, gone before the breath stopped
Mocking, mutant memories
No place for butterflies
Too fearful to sleep

My hand numb with grasping what wasn't there
I felt a tiny foot light on my forehead
"Chase me, chase me."
Fields of possibilities mimicked a thousand butterflies
Without revealing the one who called
I envied those who knew the objects of the chase lived forever
in their hands
I slept

Is she still there
Just beyond my cushion?
"Chase me, chase me."
The chase is slower now
Beyond mountain, ashram,
Bodhi tree
Always beyond, beyond
A soft brush, a light touch
Hovers, gentle beyond my reach
I sleep

# NOCTURNAL VISIT
## Kristine Limont

The light in the post-operation recovery room is ambivalent, reflecting off gauzy curtain partitions. I float in and out trying to focus on the two nurses working with such intent I feel like little more than a body acting up, being difficult. I look down and watch as their flashlights shine on blood drenched wads of cloth that drip their way to the pad at the foot of the bed. The motions are constant: soak, discard, new cloth. The nurses' concentration sounds an alarm in the recess of my foggy mind. I listen to the conversation but just catch random bits.

"...Too much... blood."

"...Need... O.R... Dr... now."

The fragments are enough to move fear into me like the IV line that fills my veins.

"Kristine," calls an Asian woman in scrubs with a soft moon face sitting by the head of my bed, her hand rests light on my shoulder. I meet her gaze. "We need to go back in, I can't do

23

another epidural, I am going to have to put you under this time with general anesthesia, ok? Do you understand?"

I answer yes, though I feel sure about nothing.

They wheel me from the near darkness to the blinding light of the O.R. It is more real now and panic slips my grasp. A man's face comes close; I recognize my surgeon and relax. He's my guy. It will be ok.

Hours later I am back to floating around the recovery room. A part of me understands the crisis is over, but I can't get to that *everything is ok* place. I feel drawn to the left side of my bed. I turn my head sideways looking into the space by me, I see her there; I study that face, trying to make her real.

"Its ok Kitsel, I'm here. You are going to be fine." My dead sister's face smiles at me, full of love and concern. I look away for what feels like a couple of minutes, then back.

"I'm still here Honey, I'm not going anywhere." She gets my eye to see that I understand.

"Five years and four months I've waited for you to talk to me. I was so angry when you left me." I think I am talking out loud, but am not certain. What I do know is that my sister feels as real by my bedside as the bed itself.

I drift. Every now and then I check to see if she is still there. Each time she is and I am reassured, free to roam the ether land I'm in. Time is outside my understanding yet it feels like hours pass and each time I look Stacy is there. Comforted and a little confused I shut my eyes on the night and am consumed in restless sleep. I'm wakened in the morning light, a team in a semi-circle around my bed, some gentle prodding and poking around for bleeding. I look to the side, to see Stacy, but she is gone, replaced by a clean scrubbed physician's assistant.

I participate little in the check up and try to decide what parts of last night were real. I choose my sister, by my side, and silently tell her I love her and am glad she came, but make it clear no matter how much I would like to see her again, I won't side swipe death to make it happen. Next time we meet it will be fun, or for good.

# THE NOTE
## Eddy Conrad Heubach

The used book shops on Adams Avenue always intrigue me. It's the smell that makes me feel at home; a paper, ink and leather scent mixed with the dust of faded memories. This atmosphere awakens my senses.

Back in the stacks of short stories I found an anthology compiled by W. Somerset Maugham. The tome crackled as I fanned the pages. Out fell a folded piece of paper. It might have gone unnoticed but it opened and spun to the floor like a butterfly. The note said:

*Dear Reader,*

*This book was given to me by my husband on our third wedding anniversary. He was a sergeant in the National Guard. When Desert Storm began he was deployed to Iraq. Three months later he died defending our freedom in Baghdad.*

*It was my goal to read every story and there were only a few to go. But now I can no longer read anything from this book without his memory flooding my eyes with tears. The stories are yours now. I hope you can read them in happiness.*

*Sincerely, MVH*

*P.S. The stories by John Steinbeck and O. Henry are my favorites.*

I refolded the note and placed it as close to the center as possible then selected a couple more books to satisfy my hunger for stories. After a brief conversation with the store's owner I made my purchase.

MVH and her husband are in my thoughts whenever I read this book.

# DAY OF DECISION
## Philip Shafer

May 1968
A Gray Morning

We held hands, fingers entwined around the big coffee cup we shared, a fond, silly intimacy from our first days of marriage when we had only one cup.

She said, "Roger." She pursed her lips in a crooked smile and pulled her shoulders together. "Roger, you're 35 years old. You have four small children. You're a full time history teacher. You've been flying those helicopters, active duty and now with the reserves, for 12 years. We needed the extra money when you started, but not now."

"I know, Christine. I know." My own smile had an angry sadness. I looked into her face and said, "Tony Yockey just got his draft notice. My best student! That kid should go so I can stay home? He's not a volunteer like me."

Christine pulled her hand away and reached up to touch my face. "Your sense of duty still tugs at you, Roger, but it's a cat and mouse game. You finished all obligations years ago. You can quit any time, but as long as you drill and draw pay with

29

the reserves, they can call you up. From the news, that could be any time now."

We exchanged a questioning glance. She stood. Her face darkened and with a calm, almost detached voice, said: "NBC News showed a video of an H-34 – just like you fly." She turned away from me and stared out the window at the dawning light.

"The helicopter sat in a jungle clearing of waist high grass. Smoke poured from the engine. The rotor blades slowed. Crewmen ran away toward the camera. The copilot hung from the left side seat waving his arm. The pilot stopped. He ran back to help the copilot. The sound of gunfire mixed with yells and shouts. The video image jerked around, a booted foot in the grass, a sweep across the sky, and down to the distant tree line. The image came into focus again on the helicopter. You could actually see bullets ripping into the fuselage, ripping at the two pilots. The shooting stopped. Some voice said, 'Oh shit!' as the camera zoomed in on the dead pilots, one draped backwards on the landing gear, the other hanging upside down out of the hatch."

"Oh, God, Chris." I leapt up and wrapped her in my arms as sobs and great heaving gasps wracked her body. "Did the kids see it?"

Recovering deep breaths, as we clung together, "No" A final deep sigh, "No, they didn't see, . . . but they know, Roger, they know." We shared an intense stare. She said, "I know the old camaraderie, loyalty to those you fly with, but you have serious doubts. You really don't believe anymore. Should I quote you?"

"You know me too well, Christine."

A quick smile that faded, and she said, "If I had a choice . . . If I ever had to choose, the very last thing in the world I want is that neatly folded flag and the nation's eternal gratitude for my great sacrifice."

I touched her hand and grinned. "Could we compromise, maybe on just a slightly brave coward, maybe a slightly wounded war hero?"

"It's not funny, Roger." She pulled away and frowned. "Since this spring, since the Vietminh TET offensive, it's evident the administration, and the generals, have been lying to us. Good God, Roger, President Johnson's not going to run for reelection! Nobody believes this is an honorable war anymore." She transferred her frown to me. "Do you?"

I sighed. "It's hard to explain."

Her look took on an edgy glare. "Try."

"My oath as an officer wasn't conditional, I'll take that war, no, I think I'll pass on this one. Chris, I accepted my commission and the risks, for better or worse."

Her face turned bland. A visible shudder shook her body. Damn. How could I have said that, used those words? She's thinking: 'Yes, another sacred vow, until death do us part'. Seconds passed. Animation returned to her face, pensive, sad, resignation. I couldn't tell.

Christine wiped at her face and said, "Call tonight at dinner time if you can. Johnny has something."

Driving up to the naval air station, Christine's description and her reaction to the news video haunted my thoughts. Late-afternoon, getting ready for my second flight of the day, pilots and crew crowded by the television set. The Secretary of Defense spoke to news reporters: "The draft for June will be increased to 48,000 men, and selected reserve units will be activated immediately."

CO pulled me into his office and said, "I've been alerted for a flash message in the next few hours. I want you with me when it comes. We may have to act immediately."

I fidgeted through that foggy afternoon flight. A touch of rosy light glowed through the mist as the sun set and I landed the H-34. Everyone not on duty was gone. I sat at the bar in the Officers' Quarters, alone. I'd finished a sandwich and just ordered my second Rum and Coke. CO came through the outer door with a curious look on his face and a message form in his hand.

 "Thanks for waiting, Roger. Here it is."

I read the classified message and then turned to my commanding officer. "They're taking our aircraft, but not us?"

"That's it. They're leaving us just two birds." He departed and I sat bemused, even piqued, at having my great moral decisions snatched from me.

At the payphone in the hall, I dialed. Christine's voice said, "Hi, it's on speaker-phone." A blabber of voices: "I used that jig-a-ma-thing the way you showed me, I finished the boat and I'll get my merit badge . . . Daddy, Daddy . . . I've got a new loose tooth. Daddy, Daddy . . . Kathy has a new puppy."

"That's great John, and, Sandy, I'll tell the Tooth Fairy to get ready."

"Can we get a puppy? . . . Daddy! Daddy . . . "

"We'll see about a dog, Callie, and, okay, Laurie honey. I'm listening."

"Are you going away, Daddy?"

A long second of silence. "No, baby. I'll be home tomorrow afternoon. I'm not going away."

# WASHDAY IN ALPINE, 1947
## Janet Gastil

After Daddy went to work, and we had our breakfast, Mama pushed our new "post-war" washing machine out of its corner in the kitchen and across the linoleum-covered floor. We weren't poor, but Mama took care of three foster children so that I would have some sisters to keep me company. Together we brought in the garden hose, two large shiny galvanized washtubs for rinsing, and two chipped, painted, dark red wooden benches to hold the two tubs. We filled the tubs with cold water from the garden hose. Then we attached the hose to the kitchen sink faucet to fill the washer with hot water. Later we used the hose as a siphon to empty the tubs and washing machine to the outdoors.

Four long white steel legs, each with a small wheel like my roller skates, supported a big white enameled tub with an "agitator" inside. A metal post attached to the side of the washer tub held up the wringer, with two rollers that squeezed the dripping clothes. The water ran back into the tub. Only Mama put things through the wringer. That's because our neighbor Mar-Lou once got her long hair caught in their wringer. Her little sister pulled out the electric plug, but not until a big patch of Mar-Lou's scalp had been ripped off, requiring repeated surgeries.

We sorted the laundry into batches, based on color, and put them in the washer, starting with the white sheets and ending with the most dirty, smelly, dark socks. Mama shoved each batch of laundry under the water with a cut-off broomstick. The agitator thrashed the dirty clothes about in the washer. We girls leaned over the tub to watch our clothes appear and disappear in the churning water and listen to the rhythmic swish and swash. We giggled when drops of soapy water splashed up to our faces.

After a few minutes of poking and agitating, Mama fed the clothes through the wringer. We rinsed the clothes twice, poking and twirling them in the rinse tubs. Mama squeezed them through the ringer again after each rinse. After the final rinse, Mama rotated the wringer out over a big wicker basket. The clothes plopped into the basket, and we carried them outside. They were compressed and wrinkled by the wringer, so we had to shake them out and try to smooth them before we hung them up to dry.

Our cotton rope clothesline was strung between two large eucalyptus trees on the west side of the house, and at an angle from there to an oak tree. We had to stretch up to reach the ropes. On the sunniest days we had to squint as we hung up the white sheets. The hot sun felt good on our backs. We used two kinds of wooden clothespins. The new fancy ones had two wooden pieces, about 4 inches long, connected by a spring to secure them to the line. With these pins the clothes were less likely to slip out and fall to the dirt. I preferred the old fashioned, one-piece clothespins, about five inches long, with a round bump on the top and a long slot cut in the bottom, because they could be used to make miniature dolls.

We four girls had two teams, one to hang the clothes on the line, and the other to bring them in for sorting, folding, ironing, and distribution. When clothes fell onto the ground, we would try to wipe off the dirt. That never worked, so we blamed the dirt on the other team. The sun shone on us and on our wet clothes. The fresh outdoor air smelled of oleander and eucalyptus. I liked to watch the clothes on the lines, the sheets billowing in a gentle breeze. Sometimes a gust of strong wind whipped the clothes around and we heard them snap sharply. In winter, our fingers got numb from handling the cold, wet clothes. In springtime, pollens from the pepper trees and wild grasses made me sneeze continuously, in the grip of hay fever, while the other girls, allergy free, laughed at me. In the wilting summer heat, Mama made us cool, fresh lemonade when we came back into the house.

# FELLOW TRAVELERS
## Laura Bottaro Costner

The elevator door opened and three homeless men followed me in. My heart skipped a beat as I nodded to acknowledge them. When the door closed I drew a deep breath and prayed for a non-stop journey to the fourth floor where I would exit.

It was a Thursday morning at a large non-profit serving the mentally ill and addicted homeless population. I was the development director headed to the administrative offices; the three men were clients going to the treatment and therapy centers located on the fifth through eighth floors. It is true that we shared a common humanity but that was not what I was thinking about. My mind was on the lock down of the building two days earlier when one of the clients went on a rampage.

By all appearances these clients were not living in one of the organization's shelters but rather on the streets. Their clothes were grimy and heavily layered, their hair matted, their faces bearded. The social workers and medical staff wore jeans and athletic shoes so that the clients would feel more comfortable.

But there I stood in my charcoal suit, silk blouse and black heels, the uniform of a fundraiser. No one spoke. The person to my left stared at the wall, the two to my right kept their eyes on the floor. I stared straight ahead surveying the scene from the corners of my eyes. Except for my cologne mixing with their body odors we were silos in a box.

The elevator stopped at the second floor but there was no one there; the person must have decided to take the stairs. The door took an eternity to close. No one moved. The men continued to stare at the wall and the floor. At last the elevator stopped at the fourth floor and the door opened. They looked up as I stepped out. I turned and nodded; each nodded in return.

News of a rampage traveled through the streets like wildfire. My fellow travelers knew how vulnerable I felt. By an unspoken agreement they offered me the protective shield of stillness.

# BALLET DREAMS
## Karen Simons

I felt I was a stranger in the class and I hope no one I know now remembers that I was ever there. Even to this day it is hard for me to deal with the shame I felt, shivering and wet, crouched down on the floor between the theater seats where I had fled to hide.

It was just a beginners' ballet class sponsored by the city's Parks and Recreation Department, but in my seven-year-old imagination it could have been a ticket to beauty, grace and happiness. The unfortunate reality was a shapeless black leotard, flat black slippers, the back-stage of the local movie theater, and the metronomic barks and claps of the teacher in time to a piano.

"First position. Second position. Third position. Stop. All right girls. And again!" The dull repetition confused me…the five foot positions, five hand positions, stretches and plies. It was not that difficult, but it was hard to imagine how they could ever combine into the sparkling, spinning images in my mind? Where was my frilly tutu? When would I get to dance on my toes?

41

Where did these ideas of grandeur come from? I doubt that my
working-class parents set me up. In fact, my father's way of
showing pride was to hand out put-downs. He always said the
reason I had been given tap-dancing lessons in Kindergarten
was because I was so clumsy. Maybe I'd become more grace-
ful by dancing? Perhaps he secretly imagined I'd follow in the
footsteps of "America's Sweetheart," Shirley Temple. Exhibit
A of that theory is an early photo of me, my stick-straight hair
coaxed into sagging ringlets.

I did like the tap dancing, even if I hadn't become the grace-
ful, perky pixie my family longed for. I got my feet to shuffle,
shuffle, shuffle and kick-ball-change to beat the band! And the
clickity, clickity, clickity, clack of my shiny black patent
leather tap shoes with the black grosgrain bows gave me sassy
satisfaction. Grandma made the sweet pink-flowered and eye-
let lace pinafore I wore for the end of year recital at the San
Gabriel Auditorium and the stage at the Los Angeles County
Fair that year. With paper and bamboo parasols to complete
our outfits, the class danced to a catchy tune popular in the
early 1950s, "If I'd Known You Were Comin' I'd've Baked A
Cake." The refrain, "howd-ya do, howd-ya do, howd-ya do,"
still echos in my mind.

Alas, I wasn't "discovered" as Hollywood's next child-star
darling, and then we moved to another town. My dance "ca-
reer" ended. But when a ballet class opportunity presented
itself a year later, I don't know who was more eager for me to
attend, my parents or me.

In the meantime I had seen a movie on a neighbor's black and
white television where a little girl dreamt she could ice-skate.
Then, without any practice, with only will and imagination,

she was able to perform glides and jumps and spins with ease and perfection. This no doubt led me to believe I could do anything I set my mind to.

So as a second grader I endured the weekly ballet classes, biding my time, until I could don my beautiful gauzy and diaphanous gown and become the beautiful Sugar Plum Fairy I was meant to be.

Was I late to class that day? Had I not felt the need to use the restroom before class began? Why was I afraid to interrupt the teacher to be excused? But during a fourth position plie, my need to pee became too much. In an instant my ballet dreams came crashing down in the form of an ugly yellow puddle on the floor beneath where I stood. No one else noticed at first. But as I bolted down the steps into the dark cavernous auditorium, my socks and slippers soggy, my humiliation blazing, the piano stopped banging time and I'm sure everyone did notice. Someone with a clean-up bucket and mop clanked by, as I willed myself to disappear.

Ages passed as I crouched there between the shadowy rows; but eventually I slipped unnoticed from the theater and made my miserable way home, alone. Cold and ashamed of having wet myself, I knew I would never be able to go back. If my Mom ever knew why I quit, she never let on.

# WILD BLUE YONDER
## Kristine Limont

Your decision to saturate in

morphine and phenobarbitol

49 days after Stace's

breakfast of yogurt, klonopin,

and darvaset threw me,

heart and soul already

cleaved and gaping, trying

to staunch the loss.

On the phone, under

blue skies, warm sun,

we're saying goodbye? Forever?

Have I bled into a Dali painting?

Realizing this is better than

gone without a backward glance

I tell you I love you, you were

a good big brother.

*All right Kris, I love you too.*

*See you in the wild blue yonder.*

# MOTHER AFRICA
## Millie McCoo

### Arrival, October 1967

T he engines decreased from a roar to a soft growl when I felt the plane dipping into its descent. My heart fluttered like a dove's downy feathers in a high wind. We were approaching Mother Africa. For the first time I would be in the land of my ancestors, the earth that nurtured the genes I inherited and supported the culture which had been stolen from us when we were kidnapped and enslaved in the New World.

The jet banked to the left and to the right as it slowly headed toward Zambia. My eyes swept over the sights below: the densely-packed trees spread out to the horizon like a field of broccoli; occasional clearings of packed reddish earth encircled by round, thatch-roofed clay huts, like mushrooms; here and there a dirt path connected some of these outposts. Just like *National Geographic* photos.

In the distance, I saw an urban landscape of beige and grey multi-story buildings crowded together. As we neared the city, tree-lined, paved streets appeared, bordered by two-story houses and large grassy backyards, some with sparkling aqua pools. You didn't see these images in stories about "Darkest Africa." We flew closely over the houses then past a broad road crawling with cars. The runway flashed into view beneath us just before the plane's tires squealed as they bounced on the tarmac.

Off my side of the plane I saw a small terminal marked "Welcome to Lusaka International Airport." There were no other planes visible. Our Alitalia was the only one this early afternoon. My pulse sped up more: *Lusaka, Zambia, at last. Africa! Mother Africa*! Through my mind ran, for the countless time, my long-held imaginary vision of dashing off the plane, stepping onto the African soil and falling to my knees to kiss the land of my ancestors. The taste of the red earth would be bitter, dusty, yet sweet. My eyes rehearsed the tears that would fall when I paid my homage.

After the jet stopped and U-turned toward the terminal, I could see people on the apron. A few men were in dark blue coveralls; most were in business suits and brightly- colored dresses. The plane drew to a halt and after the engines issued a wolf-howl whine before going silent, the people approached the plane. *How casual the Zambians are about airport etiquette*, I thought.

The blue-clad men pushed the  mobile stairs to the plane. I stood up and joined in the jostling of bodies as passengers competed to retrieve bags from the overhead bins and rushed to line up for the exit.

At the open door, I looked down to see my sister, Glenda, honey-colored and elegant in a cream short-sleeved shift, with matching open-toed pumps, her hair pulled back in a glamorous bun, coolly standing at the bottom of the steps. When we met, she exclaimed, "Welcome to Zambia!" and hugged me. As I gave her cheek a peck, I realized I would not be getting down onto my hands and knees to kiss the hot, black tarmac. My long-held dream was ruined by a manufactured hardtop. There was no soil in sight.

We turned toward the terminal and I followed the crowd. Glenda gently guided me by the elbow and said, "No, we're going this way." Off to the left was a double glass door under a sign, "VIP Lounge." I didn't really have time to process this. I knew I wasn't a VIP, I was barely out of college, but Glenda obviously knew what she was doing. Her husband was a cabinet minister in Zambia's three-year-old government. Of course, government officials were considered VIP's, so I suppose their wives were, too.

We entered an enormous room with 20-foot high ceilings and rectangular windows on the walls just under the ceiling, bathing the area in warm sunlight. On the wall facing us as we entered were two huge color photographic portraits. One I recognized, the President of the Republic, with his large, round forehead, sparkling deep-set dark eyes and straight white teeth glistening in an unrehearsed smile. The other portrait was of a bespectacled man with a thin, weasel-like face, deeply receding hairline and a smirk. He, I learned, was the Vice President. These faces would become familiar. I would see them hanging in every government and private office throughout the country, as well as in restaurants and stores, and as backdrops to TV news broadcasts.

Plush, black, over-stuffed leather chairs and couches with broad plump arms lined the walls. They were set up in square conversation groupings around low coffee tables with glass

tops and thick, dark wooden legs carved in the form of ele-
phants, leaping gazelles, and other African animals. To one
side was a long bar behind which stood a dark brown man in a
crisp white, long-sleeved jacket with a stiff Nehru collar and
gleaming brass buttons down the front.

We approached a group of Zambians perched on a couch un-
der the official portraits. There were six of them, sitting
impossibly close, thigh-to-thigh, elbow to elbow: four wom-
en, a man and an adolescent boy. The women wore white
cotton blouses with short sleeves puffed at the shoulders and
ankle length sarong skirts, dancing with color and print:
greens and blues and yellows and reds, each woman wearing a
different batik print of animals or flowers or paisley-like
shapes. Around their heads were intricately-wrapped turbans
of primary shades -- blue, yellow, red – that popped against
their complexions of chocolate brown and café-au-lait. The
man, who was pudgy, was in a grey business suit and the boy
was in a white long-sleeved shirt and brown slacks.

My sister and I sat down in the love seat at one end of the cof-
fee table next to the couch. The group watched us with grave
curiosity. One of the women, small-boned with flawless ma-
hogany skin, huge dark eyes and thick lashes and a small
button nose, stood up. She walked over to me and, with
cupped hands in front of her waist, clapped almost silently
several times, while murmuring softly. She briefly met my
eyes, took my right hand, and shook it while holding her right
arm at the elbow with her left hand as if she needed extra lev-
erage.

I would soon learn that this was a sign of respect among the
Lozi people and was used in all greetings. My sister's hus-
band was of the Lozi tribe whose homeland was the Western

Province of Zambia. This lady was his older sister, whom I would call Bonosiku (a combination of her true name, "Nosiku" and "Bo", a sign of respect placed in front of an adult's first name when addressing him or her, if they were older or more senior in social rank). She sat down and one-by-one, each of the others approached me and greeted me in the same way, without smiling. The women looked at me from bowed faces but the males averted their gaze entirely as they conducted the ritual.

I raised questioning eyebrows toward Glenda in the middle of this activity, looking for approval and she nodded with a smile. By the time I greeted the last person, the boy, I found myself holding my right elbow with my left hand. Bonosiku, I noticed, so serious at the beginning, was now smiling. The tension in my body began to release.

Glenda was married to Sikota Wina, a government official. They lived in a modern two-story home that had three bed-rooms on the ground floor with one large bathroom at the end of the hall. Upstairs were the master bedroom and a gues-troom, each with its own bath. Separate from the main house was a cottage in the backyard that had a large bedroom, bath and sitting room. Glenda said that would be my room for as long as I wanted.

When we got to the house, Sikota was waiting for us. He was a Member of Parliament (MP) as well as Minister of Infor-mation and Chief Whip of the country's sole political party, which had guided the nation into independence three years before. Tall and slender, he was handsome and dashing, a rich brown fount of energy. He told Glenda and me to get into his black Mercedes Benz, saying we had someplace to go. We dropped off my luggage and drove to the farm home of one of his MP comrades.  It was a few miles outside Lusaka at the end of a potholed dirt path that branched off the southbound Kafue Road, a paved, two-lane highway.

MP Henry Thornicroft and his wife were what was called "coloured" in southern Africa; that is, mixed African and European.  They were both what we blacks in the US refer to as red-boned:  people with deep reddish hair with freckled yellow-beige skin.  The Thornicrofts looked like brother and sister, but my sister assured me later they were not related.

After serving us tea and crumpets, the Thornicrofts gave us a tour of their farm.  In addition to growing corn and other crops, they raised pigs. When the milling hogs noticed that humans were approaching, they came dashing over to the gate of their enclosure like black and white hippos on tip-toe, their heads, ears and coiled tails flopping awkwardly, their mouths issuing cheerful squeals, which translates into "the chuck wagon's coming!"

I was thrilled to see the animals. I had developed a close relationship with pigs while I attended the University of California at Davis, where I began with a major in pre-veterinary medicine.  I worked part time in the University's Swine Barn where I developed an affection for these intelligent animals. I also trained a sow whom I named Cleopatra – Cleo for short –to show at the Yolo County Fair.  We didn't win, not surprisingly since she knocked the judge over, but I did get a blue ribbon for participating.

It only took a few minutes to realize we had not come merely for me to relive my college days. I saw Sikota pointing at one of the animals. Henry called over one of his workers who went into the pen and quickly lassoed and hog-tied one of the sows. They were all female; the boar was kept in a separate area.

"What's going on?" I asked as the protesting pig was lifted by two workers and carried toward Sikota's car.

"This is in your honor!" Sikota said. "Welcome to Zambia!"

The sow was placed inside the car trunk and after it was closed, there was some banging and squealing, then silence.

The goal of our visit accomplished, we said our goodbyes to the Thornicrofts. I was frozen with dread as we drove back into town.

## First Full Day

My first morning in Mother Africa I awoke to the shrieking of a pig begging for its life with the dull thuds of an axe on wood as backup. *Squeal-squeal – chop -squeal- chop-chop.* I leaped from the strange bed in the unfamiliar room and landed on the prickly sisal rug next to it, shaking my head to clear my confusion about where I was. It wasn't my bed and it wasn't my room in Los Angeles.

Slowly, I remembered I was in one of the ground floor bed-rooms at my sister's house in Lusaka, and something awful was happening. In a panic, I dashed to the window leading to the backyard and ripped open the curtains. Fortunately, I couldn't see the visual that went with the horrendous sounds and I jerked the curtains closed. It took 15 minutes before the torture ended and the screaming ceased. My ears throbbed and my stomach coiled in knots. I hate the idea of an animal suffering and swine can produce sound effects that would make the coldest psychopath cringe. That was obviously the pig I'd met the day before.

As I showered and dressed, I was trembling and tears streaked down my cheeks. I joined Glenda, Sikota and my niece, Mpambo, for breakfast, but only had coffee.

The day was filled with the activities of Zambian family life. Sikota's relatives who lived in Lusaka came to the house to meet and welcome me. I watched and then mimicked the Lozi greetings. The children were extremely polite and well-behaved. The adults were reserved toward me, except Sikota's sister, whom I had met at the airport. She acted as if I were an old friend. The longer I lived in Zambia, the more I realized that the people, in general, were initially reserved, but once they developed a trust in you, there was no limit to their friendship and caring.

Evening approached and the family members dispersed to their homes. As dinner time neared, friends of Glenda and Sikota came: Glenda's closest friend, the widow of a Lozi man Sikota had grown up with; the Thornicrofts; two other MPs and their wives; and Jess and Les Martin, a "coloured" man and his white Jewish South African wife, political refugees from *apartheid* South Africa. Zambia provided refuge for political immigrants from southern African countries still struggling under oppressive European colonialism: Rhodesia (to become Zimbabwe), South Africa, and the Portuguese colonies of Angola and Mozambique.

The conversation was lively and, for me, highly informative. When dinner was announced by the cook, I continued my discussion with Les Martin, as we went to the table and sat down. An endless stream of serving dishes holding mashed potatoes, string beans, corn, salads and bread were set down along the length of the table. Sikota poured wine into everyone's glass. The guests fell silent when a large silver platter full of carved meat was brought to the table and set down in the middle with grand flourish by the cook.

Sikota stood and raised his glass of wine. "I wish to welcome my beloved wife's sister, Millie, to our country. I was warmly embraced by her and my American relatives when I was on an official visit to the US two years ago. I do not presume to compete with their hospitality, but I want you to know, Millie, we're very pleased you are blessing us with your presence and hope you feel at home."

"He-ya, he-ya," the MP's said ("hear, hear" in British) and everyone stood and clinked glasses.

When I sat back down, I focused on the platter and realized what it held: the roasted remains of the pig; the one that had given up its life that morning in my name. I felt sick. But after that warm speech from Sikota and seeing the glint in everyone's eyes, I forced myself to smile , as this was obviously an honor. The meat was served to me personally by my brother-in-law. I came close to retching several times as I forked the meat into my mouth and willed myself to swallow.

The sacrifice of the pig did not ruin my stay in Zambia, although it was an unsettling start.

**Moving In**

It took me almost three months to move into my quarters at Glenda and Sikota's. My five-year-old niece, Mpambo, occupied the downstairs bedroom nearest the bathroom in the main house and I temporarily slept in a bedroom across the hall from her. The rooms were set up like one would expect in an American home of the 1960's, thanks to my sister. There was wall-to-wall beige carpeting and twin beds with nubby white spreads and fringed edges. The windows, which in my room faced the backyard, were framed by floor-length curtains of beige and brown panels that completely blacked out the room from the bright Zambian sun when closed.

When Sikota came home for lunch on my second full day in Lusaka, he told my sister that an uncle and cousin were coming with their families from the village of Lealui in Western Province, which was the Lozi homeland. He asked if I would mind moving temporarily into my niece's bedroom, so that some of the family could stay in the other two downstairs bedrooms. They would also be occupying the upstairs spare bedroom and the guest cottage. I wondered, h*ow many visitors are there?* It turned out his cousin was coming with his four children and some nieces, three in fact, as well as his wife, not to mention his father, Sikota's uncle, and *his* wife. They would arrive by train the following morning.

My niece, Mpambo, had twin beds in her room. She had yet to say more than a whispered hello to me and wouldn't meet my eye, so it would be like sleeping in a room by myself. Anyway, I wasn't in a hurry to move into the cottage, since I was still adjusting to my new environment and being in the same house with my sister would give me the sense of security I needed so far from home.

The next morning, before the guests arrived, Glenda and I checked the rooms which had been prepared by Gilbert, the "houseboy" in Zambia-speak. He had augmented the regular beds with spare cots for the smaller children.

"How long will they be staying?" I asked Glenda, as we looked over the cottage in the backyard that I would move into once the guests left.

"I don't know," she said as she swiped the chest of drawers top with an index finger.

"I mean, one week, a couple of weeks?"

"I don't know."

I checked the bathroom to make sure there were soap, towels and extra rolls of toilet paper, trying to hide my frustration with Glenda's evasive answers. There were times that Glenda could be uncommunicative. She had an active, creative mind and didn't appreciate being drawn away from her thoughts. I knew this only too well. Was she avoiding answering because I was annoying her, was it too complicated to explain?

"Why don't you ask them?" I said, hoping I hid my exasperation.

"Oh, no," Glenda replied as she stopped what she was doing and looked at me in mock horror. "Seriously, you can't ask visitors how long they plan to stay. It would be an insult. It would be like saying, 'I can't wait until you leave.'"

"Really? That's weird. I mean, how are you supposed to plan your life, if you don't know?"

"That's not what's important. The important thing is that you open your home and your larder to one and all." Glenda really did use words like "larder". I'm not sure whether it was an affectation or the influence of British English.

"They don't plan their lives like we do," she continued. "You think CPT (Colored People's Time) is bad. Hah, just wait till you see how people ignore the clock here!   And they can't fathom that this is an inconvenience. We're better off financially than they are -- Sikota's a cabinet minister, after all -- and we have servants, to boot. To them, we're rich and idle."

"But, it's not just the expense.   What about your privacy? They'll be underfoot for heaven knows *how* long!"

"Well . . ." Glenda said, with her mouth contorted in thought. "Privacy is . . . well, it's just not an issue here. People are always in the company of others. One hardly ever spends time alone. It's considered unnatural . . . even unhealthy.      So, that's not a concept that people consider here . . ." She sighed and shook her head, ". . . it's just not the same thing."

She gave one of the pillows a thump before we left to check the other rooms in the house.

"Just remember, Millie, you're not in Kansas anymore."

Sikota's relatives, the Sakubitas, arrived at the house in Sikota's official Mercedes sedan, his brother's personal Mercedes and a Peugeot driven by a cousin who also lived in Lusaka. When they climbed out of the cars, it was like watching the circus act where the clowns keep coming out of the doors of the cars in an endless stream.   Out came men and boys in beige pants and white shirts; the women wore sarong skirts, called *kangas*, and blouses; instead of elaborate turbans like I'd noticed in Lusaka, they covered their hair with simple scarves, tied at the nape. The girls had short hair that sparsely covered their scalps and wore pink dresses with cap sleeves and flip flops. The exposed parts of their legs were dry and ashy, in serious need of Jergen's or Vaseline. The heels of their feet reminded me of the photos I had seen of the parched cracked fields of Oklahoma during the Dust Bowl years. Later I would find out that in the village the children and adults usually went barefoot; the Sakubitas were shod because they had come to the city.

After Gilbert helped with the luggage and set the family members up in their rooms, Glenda took the women to the bathroom and I followed curiously. She showed them how to flush the toilet, which sent them backing up from the commode in stunned amazement. They fingered the toilet paper as if caressing a baby bird. Turning the faucets on and off in the tub and the sink, elicited "oohs and ahhs" from smiling faces. None of them would have to go to a communal water tap to fill up a metal bucket and carry it back home, balancing it on the top of her head. They asked for time to wash up after their long, dusty train trip.

We had lunch prepared by the cook, Samuel, of chicken stew, with tomatoes and onions in a rich brown sauce; nshima, the Zambian staple, a thick polenta-like, tasteless loaf made from boiled maize meal; green beans and a salad. Before we began, the cook passed around a deep metal bowl of warm water with a bar of soap and then offered the medium towel hung over his left arm. I followed the villagers' lead, washing and drying my hands.

I hadn't learned to eat in the traditional Zambian manner, having only shared meals with city dwellers. The nshima is passed around in a large bowl, and each person cuts a thick wedge of it and places it onto their personal bowl. Then they spoon some of the chicken stew around the edges of the bowl. With the right hand, it is important *never* to use the left hand, one shapes a neat round ball with nimble fingers, then forms a slight indentation with the thumb, after which they scoop up a bit of the chicken, sauce and maybe some onions with it, and plop it into the mouth.

On my first attempt, I formed a bumpy ball of nshima, trying to keep from using my left hand to make it neater. I dunked it into the sauce and placed it into my mouth. Some of the sauce dripped onto my chin before I was able to eat the ball. Two of the children giggled. One of them, an eight-year-old girl, said, "Watch," and deftly rolled a smooth ball out of a piece of nshima, gently formed a scoop in its center with her thumb, dipped up some sauce and a piece of chicken in the middle and ate it neatly. I tried again, but when I tried to press a spoon shape into the ball, the nshima split in two. This caused a table full of laughter. I had to laugh, too. *This is like learning how to play a ball sport,* I thought. The youngsters enjoyed showing me how it's done and laughed at my awkwardness and at the sauce smearing my finger tips and running down my wrists. It's amazing how clean the fingers can remain if one dines properly.

I also learned at this meal that it is not only acceptable, but expected that a person make smacking sounds with their lips as they eat. It lets the hostess know of your pleasure. This was an affront to my American manners. I was appalled when Sikota's uncle, who was sitting across from me at the long table, sat back in his chair after finishing his meal, and let out a loud, deep belch. I looked at him with what I can imagine was a deep frown. Then I looked toward Glenda at the end of the table. She was busy eating, though I know that loud burp must have been audible. A minute later, the teenage boy sitting next to me gave a burp that would put any American boy to shame. I was annoyed by what I thought were dreadful table manners.

I would become adept at eating the village way and made a great impression on Sikota's relatives, becoming dexterous in eating with my right hand without being a slob. The table sounds of burps and belches ceased to bother me. But I never felt comfortable enough to join in the chorus. Instead I complimented the hosts with words.

After lunch, the family went to their rooms to rest and Glenda and Sikota went to the living room. I, meanwhile, went to the bathroom where I sloshed onto a wet floor. The toilet paper roll was soaked, and towels were lying around in piles. Thinking there was a leak, I called out to Glenda and Sikota. They dashed to the bathroom and burst out laughing when they saw my expression. Not exactly the reactions I expected. "Don't worry," Sikota said, "Gilbert will take care of it."

"Is he a plumber, too?" I asked. This brought more laughter.

"No, a mopper," said Glenda giggling.

"It's not a leak," Sikota said between chuckles. "These are village people, used to bathing from the Zambezi River." *As if I should know?* I thought. He explained that the way they bathed was to kneel beside the tub as if it were a riverbank, they would splash water onto themselves, and soap and rinse. He reminded Glenda that she would have to explain to them later how to use the tub. She laughed and said, "Oh, yeah. I forgot to tell them that."

The visitors had much to learn. So did I.

Throughout the visit, the house was full of relatives, day and night, who came to see the visitors, to give them gifts and to take them around town. These are the times I learned more about proper greetings, which explains my reception at the Lusaka airport on my arrival day. When one enters a room of people, she is ignored, or, more to the point, she is expected to find a chair and sit quietly without interrupting the conversation; eventually, the oldest or most senior person in the room acknowledges your presence which means it is time for you to approach them and, depending on their seniority, crouch or kneel before performing the clapped, softly spoken greeting.

"*Mulu meleni, Sha.*" (Hello, sir or madam). The response is "*Ay-ni sha.*" Then, "*Nazuwa handi?*" (How are you?) "*Mazuwa handi.*" (I am fine).

Then both persons repeat "*Ay-ni Sha.*" If the person is highly respected, you address them as "*Sha-ngwei,*" the plural of "*Sha.*"

This was highly ritualized and it was important to do it correctly. After greeting the elders, you were expected to continue around the room, repeating the actions and words until you had acknowledged everyone else.

The Sakubitas had been in Lusaka for three weeks when the uncle told Glenda and Sikota that they would return to the village in a couple of days. I thought Glenda would be relieved, but instead she became agitated. This changed any plans she had for her day. As the hostess, I found out, this announcement meant that she was expected to go to the train station and buy return tickets, shop for pounds of sugar, maize meal and tea for the family to take back to the village and to purchase gifts of clothing, batteries and lanterns, as well.

The appearance of the family had changed drastically from the day of their arrival. The women now wore bright colors and turbans made of yards of printed *kitenge* cloth tied stylishly in the bouffant fashion of the city. They had begun donning a touch of lipstick. Their legs were smooth and glossy with lotion and their sandaled feet were tipped with red nail polish. The men wore long-sleeved white shirts with ties and straight-creased trousers. The day they left, Sikota told Glenda a cousin of his was planning to come to Lusaka to visit, along with his wife and six children, any day now. And so it went until the end of the year: each time guests left and I prepared to move into the cottage, new guests arrived, usually without forewarning. One always made room. The only thing missing was a registration desk.

# COWBOYS
## Suzanne Williford

M y first cowboy outfit – a black Hop-along Cassidy hat, shirt, gun belt and pistol were under the tree on my fourth Christmas. This was the first of many outfits, guns, whips and boots that I wore and played with during my childhood. I watched Hop-along Cassidy, Roy Rogers, Zorro and John Wayne on TV and pretended with my neighborhood friends. When they were not available, I rode the bottom of my four poster bed letting my imagination run wild.

Cowboys were cool. Cowgirls were dumb and didn't get to do anything fun on TV or movie screen. For that very reason, I would have nothing to do with pretending to be a cowgirl.

In the fall of each year, the rodeo would come to the Lakewood Fairgrounds in Atlanta. My daddy would take me, and we would sit in the bleachers and watch the real cowboys ride bucking horses and wrestle steers to the ground. I was in heaven when I got to select a souvenir each trip. My favorite was a cat-of-nine-tails whip that I was warned not to use on my playmates. Instead, I set lots of bottles up on a fence and I tried to wrap that whip around them and pull them off. Success doing this was hard to come by using that whip. I was much better with my lariat that I had gotten in a previous year.

Time passed and I grew up, married, had children, divorced and went along without thinking about cowboys. Then all of a sudden my world turned upside down. I met a real cowboy. Sure, he had another job, but on the weekends, he was a rodeo cowboy. I could live in the world of my youth once again.

BJ was a bronc rider. He grew up on a horse ranch in Utah and had been rodeo-ing since he started riding calves at the age of five. He left home at thirteen and rode professionally. He progressed up the chain and rode and roped just about anything with four legs. He broke horses on ranches during this time, so he knew a lot of horse psychology too. This helped him to stay on horses a little longer in the ring.

I began traveling with him every weekend to a rodeo event. I became very comfortable in my jeans and cowboy boots that I climbed onto horse fences with. Although I'm sure I must have looked like a citified cowgirl, I could still play the part. I went behind the chutes and helped with the bindings and getting BJ set on the various broncs before his rides. When he got that C-curled spine position, chin down and hat secured, he nodded to the guy opening the chute door and the horse would literally bolt into the arena.

Sometimes he would win and be awarded a new belt buckle, sometimes he would place, and sometimes he would get hurt and need me to drive back home. While the finish mattered to him, I didn't really care about the outcome. I was getting to spend time with my handsome, strong cowboy and live out a childhood dream.

As with most situations rooted in fantasy, and after many rodeos, it all came to an end. I did not get to continue spending time with my cowboy. Had I been pretending all those years? Maybe. Did I get my heart broken? Yes. Would I do it again? You bet! Once a year, I still polish those same Tony Lamas and reflect on the good times and the big love of my life.

## SHAPE SHIFTING MAMA
### Kary Lynn Vail

*D*ear Jane,

    *Enclosed is my application to join your "Get Over It & Get On With It" club.*

*Qualifications: Over fifty, post menopausal, single, and manic depressive.*

*Sex life: Very active in memories of things past. Quietly benign in anticipation of things to come.*

*Physical Fitness:* I thought a long time about that one before writing: *when I walk by the mirror in the buck and glimpse the nether-lands of my anatomy, I think Freak Show Fat Lady.*

How does Darlene Shiloh manage to look so svelte?

I sighed, signed and sealed the letter, set it aside for mailing, and then collapsed on the bed. Another spring twanged in surrender. I sagged a little further.

It came to me.

I'm *"over the hill."* I couldn't see my toes. I couldn't see any
of me beyond the rise of my belly. That's *"over the hill."* But
I knew all those necessary parts were there. I could feel them,
and I could feel the civil war between my thighs.

First. I started walking like John Wayne, now it's the side-
step-poop-waddle as my inner thighs rasp at each other like
two giant sticks making a boy-scout fire.

Phat girls, share the wealth! It took forever for someone to tell
me to lotion and powder those private parts. Life saver.

And shape-wear. Huh, 'nuff said.'

Number one. Do not pack or wear virgin shape-wear that has
not had a road test.

Two. Don't ever test drive shape-wear alone, *sans* an extrac-
tion team.

Next day, I caught the mailman – ugly as sin but looking bet-
ter all the time. He took my letter to "Dear Jane" and handed
me one from my dear step-daddy treating me to a spa retreat in
Ixtapa, Mexico. Behold my woeful saga.

Gussying up for a low fat dinner under tropical stars, I pulled
out a sleek, black industrial shape-wear for that "Big Sexy"
look I was fixing to flaunt. My new untried shape-wear was a
stretchy, constricting toilet-role tube topped off with a silky
slip sheath designed to mask rolling, effervescent waves of
muffin top.  Stem to stern coverage—ass, belly, tits. I stepped

into the black hole and attempted to pull the shaper up over the fountain of my hips. Not happening.

Next, my last resort for hippy phat girls, was to pull the shaper off and go over the top—the ol' *Head vs. Ass* fail proof route. On a Jihad, I mugged my head with the black shaper enveloping me in a dark world of suffocation. My arms were straight up beside my ears reaching for the ceiling in goal post position.

Attempting to breathe and see, I fretted, sweated and shimmied the shape-shifting-squeezer over my neck. Now I could neither breathe nor see. Gushing perspiration and my make-up commenced creating a shroud of Turin on the shaper as the silky outer layers slid up to cover my elbows -- one of my few parts where bones revealed themselves.

Arms locked straight up in the air, the Spandex quicksand took its awesome toll. A bent over L-shaped-she-Frankenstein, I twiggled my fingers using the tentacles as feelers and crashed into the floor lamp that subsequently served as a metronome whose to and fro resulted in my being beaned on the noggin. Once I stopped the lamp stand's abuse, I tripped over the cord and fell on the coffee table. Alone in the hotel room, shaper for a head, I was a careening black missile lost in space.

Desperate, I began to use the antennas of my arms to touch and feel the crap I was falling over. Tripping on my three-and-a-half-inch-heel pumps, I staggered back and face-planted the television set. Ricocheting, I belly-flopped on the bed with such velocity that I bounced off the mattress dragging the coverlet over me on the floor. Unable to pull the bedspread off of me, my attempts to escape rolled me up like a pig in a blanket.

Worm-like I scooted in vain to liberate myself.

Resigned, I went along the perimeter of the mattress for the nightstand. I'll dial for the front desk, maybe get help. In-and-out of down-dog position, I mushed towards my goal.
Bingo! The night stand. Dizzy I sat up for air banging the hell out of my noggin again on the lip of the night stand. Domino effect, my Diet Coke spilled, running down the tube-shute to my head then torso.

I waved my hands for help up and down like a cork screw till my shaper cupped my tits in a chokehold bouquet. Once the Spandex passed my elbows, I grabbed the shaper with my hands and commenced a bionic Taffy pull. Gather, pull, gather pull! The shaper snagged on every ridge, roll and valley of fat. All at once the shaper gave way. Wriggling and wrangling I headed face first toward the ocular of light stemming from the light fixture. Shaper off, I flopped, spent, on the rug.

A recovering breath. Yes, 'nuff said.' Rising. The mirror again. My pathetic reflection. My studiously applied make-up, now one big sweaty smear.

A skunk stripe of Carnelian lipstick ran up my nose to my forehead. Matching red blood oozed where my right-pierced earring had snag-shorn my ear lobe. Rug burns adorned my hands and knees.

I appraised my naked body, the rolly-hula hoops of flesh that began under my boobs and ended in a mini-skirt over those unseen parts. What the Hell, it's me in all my abundant glory.

Chanting to myself, "What would Dear Jane do?" I showered,

lotioned, powdered, and applied matching band aides to my ears. Donning a *tres chic* Muu Muu, I made my grand entrance to the dining room as heads turned and admiring glances followed me.

# OUT OF THE BLUE
## Kristine Limont

Outside of good public radio, concerts, and the occasional tab of LSD, Durham, New Hampshire, was not a happening place for teenagers. When mom asked my sister Stacy and I to go with her to Concord where she was teaching a class we thrilled her by saying yes. She didn't need to know we'd only agreed because it seemed less boring than staying home.

The sixties were over, but there was still plenty of traffic on the Metaphysical Highway. We had traveled this road *a lot* with my mom: Sufi dancing, faith healers, and macrobiotic diets. It had gone from exotic to dull faster than one could say *Be Here Now*. During the hour car ride she chattered about her new crop of students while Stacy and I added a word here and there as needed, the landscape slowly changed from rural to urban.

My mom was currently an instructor of *Silva Mind Control*. Her seminars were taught over two weekends, though I always thought it came down to a few mental exercises, which certainly did not take four days to learn. But I had noticed people

in these kinds of workshops seemed to need the same infor-
mation told many times in different ways.

We pulled into the motel parking lot and I was immediately
bummed by its small size. It didn't even have a valet or semi-
circle out front for unloading, just pick a space, pull in, and
lug your stuff inside. My hope for a large place full of interest-
ing nooks to ferret out dissolved. The building's arms shot off
the center like stubby fingers. The lobby was carpeted in a
shade of red favored in the seventies: non-descript and unin-
viting. The air wore *Eau de Cigarettes* and tinny music leaked
from somewhere.

Stacy and I stayed in the room while our mom went to care for
her incoming students. We faced each other from matching
double beds.

"What do you wanna do?" Stacy asked, watching as I blew
neat smoke rings into the air.

"I don't know, I guess we could go have a look in the class,
see if there are any cute guys, or we could explore this dump."
We opted for beefcakes.

We entered the conference room, ignored the quizzical looks,
and sat in the back like we owned the place. Our smugness
was good until my mom paused her instruction and introduced
*her daughters* to the group. Now we wanted to leave, but felt
like we *had* to stay. After all we had just interrupted every-
thing and to get up and go so soon felt rude even to us.

We entertained ourselves for a couple of hours trying quietly
to make each other laugh. We were in that state of boredom
where everything seemed hilarious. We managed not to laugh
out loud, but still drew threatening looks from Mother Teach-

er. When break time was called we made a speedy get away, or as speedy as two people with Muscular Dystrophy could make. Stacy walked with a swaying stride on the toes of her feet. I walked like a doll whose knees wouldn't bend at the same time, a Tin Man gait.

We found vending machines, bought some candy, explored all the main hallways; nothing exciting going on anywhere.

"What were we thinking? This sucks!"

"Yeah" Stacy answered, "let's go over that way, looks like an indoor pool."

We entered the room, the temperature like a summer day after a rain that heats rather than cools. The smell of chlorine was so thick I imagined it filling my lungs, turning them green. We stood for a moment and took in the scene. It was desolate. A hand full of frumpy adults were busy by the far corner of the pool, laying towels on lounge chairs and shoving brightly colored bags underneath them.

"Wanna go check out the water?" Stacy asked, though we both knew it would be too much work to bend over and feel the inviting blue liquid. We walked to the edge of the shallow end anyway.

Movement in the water pulled my gaze over and I gave Stacy a jab in the ribs. "Holy crap" she said as I collapsed to the ground dropping my arm into the pool as far as I could. While I acted without thinking, my fifteen-year-old ego found its voice and declared how *stupid* I looked and that it was going to be *really hard* to get back up. The little girl bounced on her toes, fingers stretched to break the water's surface. Her frantic eyes locked onto mine and wouldn't let go. I leaned in further and she grabbed my hand. I pulled her up over the edge of the pool and held her close as her shrieks echoed off the tile walls. Water dripped and puddled around us. The adults rushed over and a woman grabbed the child from me, glaring like *I* had pushed her into the pool. No one said thank you, asked what happened, or if I was okay, they just whisked the girl back to their camp.

I moved onto my hands and knees, straightened my legs until I was folded in half, palms pressed on the ground. Then I walked my hands up my legs and finally righted myself.

"Nice." I said.

"No shit." Stacy said as shades of disgust crossed her face.

We turned and left the steamy room. A few steps later Stacy stopped and turned to me, the full impact of what just happened dawning on her, "You saved that girl's life!"

I thought about this. Had I? Surely someone would have noticed she was missing, but what if they hadn't? Or realized it too late? I rolled this idea around in my head, looked for feelings. I felt good about what I'd done. Yet the darkness, the fear I had fought hard to suppress, heated like lava called to the sea. Nobody had explained things to me, but I'd listened to my mom explain it to the Highway Hawkers she met on her quest for answers. I'd gleaned enough. I had a muscle disease. Incurable. Progressive. Panic had been kept at bay in hope the cure was out there and mom would find it. She still searched but I had reverted to fear, which I'd sealed up tighter than Poe's black cat. Until today. Now my darkness flowed out, pulled into the soup of the girl's nightmare.

"What's wrong?" Stacy asked as we ambled back to our room.

"Nothing. I don't know, it just feels kind of weird." I deflected.

I replayed the incident in my head. The adults acted hostile towards me. I found I didn't care. It was those eyes full of desperation that had moved me to act. Screw the adults, what did they know and how come no one was watching her? I felt good, like a toasty blanket warmed my insides. That girl would know. She would remember. That was enough. It made me feel like I had loaded my boat full of good karma I could draw on forever. If I did nothing else with my life, I had at least saved a little girl. Even if no hand was coming for me.

## THE NURSING HOME
### Barb Huntington

In mid-October, the El Cajon Valley of inland San Diego blows dry with the Santa Ana winds. Darkness comes early and with it the first chill nights. As I descended into the hazy dusk, my headlights joined a sinuous river disappearing past a giant granite outcropping, still reflecting the last of the red sunset.

Other drivers sped by, eager to get home to warm dinners as I poked along in the slow lane from my job at the university. Eventually I had to turn off, past the strip malls, the liquor store, the 50s tract houses, to turn into the parking lot of Magnolia Manor.

My vision of a stately southern mansion contrasted sharply with this mishmash of stucco and glass. A pine and a shaggy palm rose above the cracked pavement and dead grass. The liquid amber trees had already felt the evening cold, their leaves in last red scream before the dry wind sucked their life and color and left them brown and crumpled on the asphalt. By the door an early jack-o'-lantern that wouldn't see Hallow-

een succumbed to mold. Lid gone, its bouquet of chrysanthe-
mums added to the slime.

My steps slowed as I stared at the glass panes in the door and
reflected on the weary grey-haired women backlit by the lights
from the industrial complex across the lot. Taking a breath I
yanked the door open and imagined an audible sigh from the
moist air that had been waiting to escape. As I pulled the door
closed behind me, more damp heat tried to smother me with
the heaviness of overcooked vegetables and pasta, adult dia-
pers yet to be changed, the rancid odor of old people that
could not be covered by the overpowering lilies where I
signed in. I tried not to stare at the desiccated bodies lined up
in wheelchairs before me, but their eyes were on me. Accus-
ing eyes, prisoner's eyes, eyes that no one lived behind. They
hated this place, but they were part of it and their eyes branded
me as an intruder. Fred was not amongst them.

I signed in and walked through the halls, past the cage of
scruffy, luckless finches and a woman with swollen ankles
who sorted medications at her stainless steel cart. I glanced in
the common room, the battered grand piano in the corner.
Four days ago, when they brought Fred here from the hospital,
he made a beeline for that piano. For a moment he forgot his
shaky Parkinson's hands to pound out a Beatles tune. When
the manor matron's intent on Mahjong at a distant table yelled
that he was disturbing their game, I realized that at sixty-
seven, he was too young for that crowd. The bossy women
were in 'their' room now. He wasn't.

It has been a hard transition. The second day he gamely went
to bingo and gallantly stood up for a confused old lady clutch-
ing a teddy bear they barred from playing. The old biddies

hated Fred and he knew it. He threatened their final domain. Fred, the elementary school principal everyone loved. I tried to get him into a better nursing home. I visited some beauties and they all had openings until I applied officially and they figured out my strategy to pay full price upfront and then go on MediCal.

After twelve years of holding a full time job and caring for Fred and his cadre of little children hallucinations at night, I was tired. When one morning I found him unresponsive, his oxygen off and melted ice cream all over the house, I sighed, reattached the oxygen cannula to his nose and called the nursing hotline. No, I didn't just call 911 because I had called them so many times in the past only to have him sent home again. I felt I needed support in my decision. By the time the paramedics arrived, Fred was awake, his oxygen levels were almost normal. It took a little convincing to have them take him once again to emergency. To their credit, he had called 911 more than once when his hallucinations told him that I needed help and was caught in the chair he had turned over. At the hospital I overheard one doctor tell another that the only reason Fred was there was because I wanted to have him committed to a nursing home. Fred was responsive, talkative, lucid, and I had to get my kids on my cell phone to convince him to remain for observation. The staff continued to blame me as a conniving woman until the sun went down and Fred told them he was holding hostages in his room to keep the cops from taking him for some unnamed crime.

The next day I visited nursing homes and carefully analyzed each one until I whittled it down to the only one that would take him. By the end of the week Fred and his hallucinations were on their way to Magnolia Manor by ambulance while I followed behind, attempting to find positives, like the grand piano, to point out to him.

Now I entered his room where he sat in his lounge chair, the oxygen tube around his neck, not in his nose. I assumed it had not touched the floor so I gently replaced it and asked if the nurse had brought his meds. He didn't think so but wasn't sure. When his food tray came in, he was shaking so hard that I had to feed him while he told me how the children in the corner were laughing at him. He coughed up a large, green glob which I caught with a tissue and lobbed into his over-flowing wastebasket. Now I knew why the air was so moist. There was probably a wastebasket like this in every room. Each inhabitant was filling tissues with snot, tears, and large masses of coughed-up phlegm. Having lived with Fred's deni-zens for years, it was easy for me to visualize every resident of the ambitiously named manor filling tissues and wastebaskets as they, themselves, dried and shriveled and eventually disap-peared.

As I shoveled in food, Fred suddenly looked at me with his Parkinson's 'deer-in-the-headlights' look, closed his eyes, and snored. I wish I could remember if I kissed him goodnight be-fore I tiptoed out to the nurses' station to find out about his meds and to remind them to check his oxygen. I entered the pass code and let myself out the door. Stepping carefully to avoid the now totally collapsed pumpkin, I pulled the cool de-licious air into my lungs and kept the car windows down on the half hour drive home.

As I entered the dark house, our old dog whined softly. I fed her, stroked her soft head, downed a bowl of cereal and went to bed. About 10:30 pm, I surfaced to my ringing phone. "We called 911, he is in ER. Unresponsive." Driving back on the empty, dark freeway, windows closed against the cold, I wondered if he had removed his oxygen cannula and if it had fallen on the dirty floor. I fantasized the manor matrons as witches sneaking into his darkened room and gleefully removing it, perhaps aided by the evil little children in the corner. At the hospital I saw x-rays of his filling lungs. They had been clear when he left the hospital. The family gathered but Fred never regained consciousness. Would he have lived if I had found the strength to keep him home just a little bit longer? Death by nursing home. How many others have been killed by Magnolia Manor? Like the jack o' lantern, he didn't make it to Halloween.

# WALL STREET: DIMES, DOLLARS, 25-CENT POOLS
## Laura Bottaro Costner

L ady, why don't you go shopping and buy yourself a new dress!" Slam went the phone. So went my first experience with the New York over-the-counter (OTC) trading desk as a rookie stockbroker. With the receiver dangling off a fully extended arm, I blurted out, "He hung up on me. How can he do that? I'm a broker and I used to be a teacher." We didn't have private offices back in the 1980's. We worked in a large room called a 'bullpen'. It consisted of 30 desks for 30 brokers with a ticker tape running across the front of the room. My eyebrows started to come down when I heard laughter all around me and I too realized how ridiculous my outburst. I joined in the laughter, what else?

Humiliated or not I needed to get the option quotes and call my client back. I asked a colleague who did a lot of option trading to place the call for quotes while I listened intently and took notes. Instead of my sing-song ramble about a client who wanted the price for particular options, I heard something akin to military 'name, rank and serial number' jargon. No wonder the trader hung up on me. They were taking calls by the minute and he knew he was a dollar waiting on a dime.

I communicated well with clients and knew my products and services. As a former teacher, that was the easy part. What I learned on the job was Wall Street protocol and culture. The next time I called the trading desk I took a deep breath and in rapid fire I identified myself and office location, stock, strike price, expiration date, number of contracts, phone number. Response? "You got it. Call you back in 15 minutes."

There was another bit of culture I came to know and that was the 25-cent rookie pool. A take-off on baseball and football pools, it worked like this. When new brokers came on board, the veterans would place their name and the rookies' name on a calendar—then throw 25 cents into the pot. With failure rates of 85% in the first three years, they were picking a date when each new broker would go south. The veteran who had the date closest to the person's actual date of departure won the pot.

The rookie pool and the whole idea of betting on failure was a cultural shock but it was also a great motivator. Instead of being insulted or in any way devalued, I made a vow, 'They're not going to get me'. And they didn't. At the end of my first year I made Executive Club and retired from the industry as a certified financial planner thirty years later. I had to admit to some truth in one veteran's explanation on why there is no difference between a sports pool and a rookie pool, "Those who do well survive, those who don't are eliminated."

# A NICKEL IN MY HAND
## Janet Gastil

My sunsuit didn't have pockets so I clutched the big silver coin with the picture of an Indian in my hand. I knew it was the same as five whole pennies, and I knew it was enough for an ice cream cone. Frankie had told me. He was nine and lived with us in Floral Park. He was supposed to watch out for me when Mama was busy.

We were at Jones Beach, my favorite place. Mama had a client who let us stay at her cottage, instead of paying her. The cottage had a porch all around it with a wooden floor, wooden railings, and eight wooden steps down to the boardwalk. We could take that boardwalk along the beach all the way to the ice cream store.

Mama was busy with a client. Frankie was reading a comic book. I was 4 1/2 years old. I had a nickel, and I knew what to do with it. I started from the wooden porch, and down the steps to the boardwalk. My sandals clicked loudly with each step.

It was farther than I remembered, but I found the ice cream store and I gave the clerk the nickel I had held tight in my hand all the way. "Vanilla, please," I said.

"Are you all by yourself?" He gave me a look like half-smile and half-frown.

"Yes. Mama has to work. I like ice cream."

He handed me a big vanilla ice cream cone. "Does your mother know where you are?"

"She knows I'm at Jones Beach."

"That's good. What's your name?"

"My name is Emily. But everybody calls me Janet."

"What's your last name?"

"Manly. I'm Janet Manly. We're staying at the dark brown cottage with a porch that goes all the way around. I'm going home now. Goodbye."

The ice cream tasted sweet and creamy. It came in a tall cone, pointed at the bottom, with a round ball of white ice cream at the top. I ate slowly, licking up drops that melted and tried to run down the side of the cone and make my fingers sticky. I finished my ice cream and kept on walking back along the boardwalk. I was almost back to the cottage when I saw Mama and Frankie running toward me.

"Where have you been? What are you doing?" Their faces had that scolding look. "We were worried about you!"

"What does 'worried' mean?" I asked Mama.

"It means we were afraid something bad might have happened to you," Frankie answered.

"I walked up the boardwalk to buy an ice cream cone, with my nickel."

Mama said, "We're going to have a talk about this when we get home. It's almost a mile to that grocery store. We didn't know where you were."

I wasn't happy about having a talk. That meant sitting in an uncomfortable straight-backed chair and listening to Mama talk about what I had done wrong.

Back at the cottage, Mama said right away, "You get on this chair," so I climbed onto a plain wooden chair in the kitchen.

Mama began talking. "You must never, never go out alone without permission."

I'd heard that word, "permission," before. I knew I was in trouble when I heard that word.

"Frankie told me you showed him a nickel and asked if it was enough to buy ice cream. That's how we guessed where you went. We started up the boardwalk to look for you, and you're lucky we found you before dark. If we hadn't found you on the boardwalk, I would have called the police. "

"Can I get off the chair now?"

Mama said, "First promise me that before you go out again, you will ask for permission. Then you may get up."

I wasn't so sure about asking permission. Mama seemed to think it was important, so I said, "Okay," and agreed to do it, next time.

.

# DINNER WITH JIZO
## Barb Huntington

Jizo smiles across my plate

Watches me pause, a cube of tofu

Pressed against my lips,

I spear a sprig

Of still crunchy broccoli that

Grew in my garden

An hour before.

Through a glass of red wine, I peer back at Jizo,

Note the tear in his left eye

A bit of coconut oil?

Your tear is fading, I say,

It seemed to appear when my tiny grandson moved in.

Was that too much to bear, protector of mothers and children?

Jizo smiles, silent, surrounded by shiny rocks,

That once garnished the desk where I counseled future healers

I point my cell phone camera at plate and statue,

Snap a picture

Post.

Return, now, to savor deep green spinach, shameless red and white Chioggia beets

Garish orange carrots,

A bit of brown rice.

When the bowl is clean,

Jizo smiles,

"Are you going to eat that square of dark chocolate?"

# WALKING BEHIND A LITTLE OLD LADY
## Millie McCoo

She is so tiny, her movements so slow and tentative.

I broaden my stride to get around

 this black-cloaked impediment to my progress,

with its exaggerated hump rising between bent shoulders

and the scraggly, gray wisps of hair

Splaying out from beneath the little black cap.

Her handbag hangs limply by two thin straps
in the crook of her bent right arm;

the crepey skin drapes from twig-like bones.

In her left hand, a thick wooden cane

which she taps tremulously onto the hard,

gray, unyielding sidewalk, like a third leg

as useless as the thin, shod limbs

that shuffle her along,

slow as drifting glaciers.

As I draw nearer, I marvel:

How easy it would be to trip her --

hearing the crunch and crackle of brittle bones

as she hits the pavement --

and snatch the handbag from her withered arm.

How dare she interfere in this bustling street.

She is so fragile,

a charade of independence.

She belongs inside, behind deadbolt locks and chains,

in front of the TV

safe and invisible.

I slow my pace and imagine

approaching her,

and gently cupping her bony elbow

in my firm right palm, guiding her,

while stroking the velvet crinkled skin of her arm

and whispering questions.

I stop.

I ponder her retreating back

as she hobbles into the distance

with my future.

## ENGLAND: THE FOUR SEASONS
### Laura Bottaro Costner

S now flurries greeted Harry and Jeanne when they stepped off the train in St. Albans, the historic city that would be their home for the next year. It met all their criteria for the perfect place to experience the four seasons while they completed a writing project. The population of 100,000 included few tourists, historic architecture defined the city, London was only twenty miles away in case Harry needed to access research facilities and they were able to lease a modern townhouse. With a publisher's deadline of October they set to work immediately on transforming Harry's dissertation into a book. Whenever they needed a break from rewrites, they explored various sites and used their imaginations to travel back in history. All year long, the changing seasons determined where they went as well as where they lingered. They discovered that there was far more to English weather than rain and low hanging mist.

On arrival they decided to shop European-style which to them meant a walk every few days to the green grocer, the butcher shop, the bakery and, on Wednesdays, the farmer's market vibrant with the colors of seasonal flowers and the sounds of hawkers. Jeanne thought it would do them both good to carry grocery bags on the walk back and forth. Fresh bread, butter and English white cheddar cheese became staples in their diet making the exercise a necessity. In January and February they suited up with layers, hats, woolen scarves, and fleece lined gloves to face the bitter damp cold that cut right through them. The sidewalks were paths with 6 to 8 inches of snow on each side and the chill outlined their every breath. It's no surprise that most trips involved a stop at a tea shop or pub on George Street, the Tudor-style high street that, in an instant, transported them back to the days of Henry VIII. Harry came up with pop quizzes like "Name the three kings that came before, and after, Henry VIII." Jeanne always wondered if Cromwell ever strolled down the winding high street while carrying out Henry's order to dissolve all the abbeys. More than likely he did.

Work on the manuscript progressed on schedule and the old market town delivered on all their expectations but, though the snow flurries ended, the first week of March brought little change in the weather. Menacing skies and rain prevailed; countless days of cold air still penetrated their warmest clothing. Harry seemed to be going through his scotch a little too quickly; he and Jeanne argued about that. "It's only 2:00." "Yes but the walk home was freezing, downright bone-numbing." Then Jeanne came down with the head cold of a lifetime. The winter weather convinced them it was time to end their experiment of living *sans* auto. Harry bought a used VW Bug for 400 pounds and they discovered Tesco, the local supermarket. As they drove out of the car park, Jeanne confessed, "At the butcher's shop, I always felt foolish when I had to describe with my hands how many pounds I wanted." Harry quipped, "Yeah well, besides, all busy people shop in supermarkets." And so they did. With a car they were also able to travel farther afield. A few miles away was Hatfield House where Elizabeth 1 spent her childhood. Every few weeks they skipped the tea shops to travel out to Hatfield House for lunch. On sunny days they walked the gardens listening for lutes. They never heard them and decided winter was the wrong season for lutes.

Time passed and the sun made its appearance for longer stretches. Daytime temperatures rose a few degrees and the outdoors beckoned especially when words didn't flow and the writing stopped. Time to take a break. Buds on the trees were bursting; spring was in the air. Patches of tulips and daffodils brought color everywhere. Throughout the town medians that divided traffic also served as flower beds. Every six weeks or so they would be filled with seasonal flowers with brilliant color the main criterion for inclusion. Early spring was no exception. As soon as the tulips started to fade, new colors appeared in ever more varieties of blooms. It was a perfect time to climb the hill to St. Albans Cathedral which they did numerous times. On one occasion Jeanne looked around to find Harry some ten paces behind her, his head cocked to the right and his gaze fixed in the distance. Lost in history, Harry imagined the stampede of horses and the clash of swords from the first battle of the War of Roses in St. Albans in 1455. More quizzes; "Which side represented Henry VII, the House of York or the House of Lancaster?" Jeanne had reviewed English history before the trip and was quick to answer, "Lancaster defeated York and began the Tudor line with Henry VII. York and Richard III were out." When they returned to the Abbey the next Saturday morning, the imagined War of Roses had given way to battling soccer (football) teams, cheering parents and referees' whistles, making it difficult to lose oneself in history. Jeanne found it the perfect moment to quiz Harry. "So, professor, where was the Magna Carta drafted?"

Distracted by the matches, Harry answered in a flash, "Runnymede."

"Nope. It was signed at Runnymede but drafted right here in St. Albans Abbey." Jeanne took delight in besting Harry as he was at one time her professor. "I think I just won a nice lunch." He agreed. She picked St. Alban's oldest pub 'Ye Olde Fighting Cocks,' one of four contenders for the title of 'oldest' pub in Britain.

Spring came and went and summer did arrive, finally. They went to their first cricket match which they pretended to understand after it was explained to them a second time by friends. They just kept nodding so as not to appear too dull. They took short day trips to surrounding towns and villages, Hemel Hempstead, Potter's Bar, King's Langley and always to a new pub for lunch. Harry planted a vegetable garden that produced in abundance. The neighbors were happy to share the giant cucumbers, the zucchini and, of course, more tomatoes than any two people could eat. Work on the book continued in earnest but it took discipline to keep at it. The brilliant blue skies and shady tree-lined lanes just wide enough for a VW Bug were genuine competition. However, a challenge more daunting than meeting the publisher's October deadline presented itself at the end of July. Jeanne discovered a lump in her breast. A hard little mass that felt like a BB. Long before it became a popular slogan, 'Keep Calm and Carry On' was her go-to reaction to the unexpected. For two days she went back and forth quietly weighing her thoughts, 'If I have to have chemo, we'll never finish the book on time' and

'Mid-October is only 10 weeks away, what if I hadn't discovered it until then?' She made a decision. Ignore the lump and continue to work on the manuscript so it would be ready on time. When she told Harry what she had decided, he quoted his seventy-two hour rule. "Never make an important decision with less than 3 days consideration." She thought about it for another day. No change. She would stay the course.

They continued to poke around the sites and shops when they needed to clear their heads and one day came across an old map in a used bookstore. That was how they found ancient paths with names like 'Old Watling Street'. Paved over by the Romans in 45AD it connected Verulamium, the Roman city that became St. Albans, to other parts of the empire. They paid a visit to the Verulamium Museum and walked around what remained of the ancient city. But summer, with temperatures in the mid-80s, was not the time to explore Roman ruins. They had no hats to block the sun and the humidity was higher than normal. Even though Jeanne was good at compartmentalizing, the heat made her irritable and thoughts of the lump vied for her attention. She became downright cranky on the ride home. "No, I don't want to stop at a pub," she snapped. Once home, Harry cranked up the AC and poured a couple of cool ones. Next he went to the stack of travel brochures left by the landlord and pulled out those featuring Britain's southern coast. "I think we need a change of scenery," Harry suggested. Without hesitation, she agreed. A week later they packed-up all their papers and headed for the cooler climate of Cornwall. Summer showers tended the garden while they were away.

Fall rolled around and the weather turned crisp and, to them, perfect. A carpet of yellow gold leaves beneath copper and orange oak trees are autumn's calling card in England. The skies remain blue and serve as a backdrop for patches of in-termingled grey and white clouds.

At 10:00 on a cool, breezy Wednesday morning in mid-October they delivered the manuscript to the post office. At 11:00 Jeanne went to see a doctor. She worked a "Reader's Digest" puzzle as she waited for the charge nurse to call her name. The crowded hallway lined with chairs was like a cat-walk. Each time a name was called, all eyes followed the patient down the narrow walkway. Jeanne was so engrossed in her word puzzle that she didn't look up until the third call of her name, a Slavic name that was so mispronounced it came out 'catch-a-witch'. She overheard one woman comment to another, "Poor girl with a name like that." 'Right. Keep Calm and Carry On'. After the exam they ran some tests and told her to wait for the results. When the charge nurse called her back into a patient room, she listened quietly as the doctor told her "The results are suspicious." Her eyebrows arched and she tensed-up when she was instructed to report for surgery at seven the next morning.

On the way home, she stopped in at Marks and Spencer to purchase a robe and slippers. She thought that must be what the nurse meant by "Go home and get ready for tomorrow morning." Normally a very private person, Jeanne felt driven to tell someone about the surgery besides Harry. She invited herself for tea with Margery, the older woman who lived next door. They had chatted a half dozen times about travel and English gardens so she felt a bond. Jeanne opened the con-versation with news about the surgery and talked in detail about the events of the day. Not until Robert, Margery's hus-band, knocked on the door saying, "I thought you were going to a luncheon," did Jeanne notice that her hostess was dressed up to go out. Margery never said a word but instead kept smiling at Robert until he realized that she must have decided otherwise. He quietly closed the sitting room door. When the tea and biscuits were finished Jeanne thanked Margery and apologized for keeping her from her plans. Margery replied, "I was exactly where I wanted to be this afternoon." Visiting with Margery was the best thing she did to prepare her mind for surgery. When Harry backed the car out of the driveway at six-thirty the next morning, their neighbor, Margery, was busily tending her front garden. She heard the sound of the engine and spun around with a smile and a hearty thumbs-up. That good luck gesture paid-off. The lump was benign.

With work and worry behind them, Harry and Jeanne heard London call—museums, Selfridges, theaters, pubs and festive holiday lights. A friend of Harry's offered them an apartment for November and December, a small apartment with no central heating. They would have to make do with a coin-operated space heater. They would have to bundle up again when the cold weather returned, as it surely would. Harry could pour himself an extra stiff one or two and Jeanne could feed the heater. They would manage. Their journey for all seasons was about to come full circle.

# I WANT TO BE KING
## Kary Lynn Vail

Disco. Harvey Milk. Planned Parenthood. I looked at the sign-in sheet arrival column - 1:45, appointment time - 1:15.

"Ugh"

The sliding glass window opened . . . Sesame . . . and a honey colored arm examined the clip board.

Thumbelina eyes rolled up and gave me the "tsk-tsk," look.

"Your late.  Take a seat."

"Sha-link." The window slid shut.

Sizing-up Planned Parenthood, I pegged round the waiting room, pigeonholing the clientele: A hand-holding, pimple-faced boyfriend, pregnancy test, birth-control first-timer, yeast infection, a wild-carder who didn't look good, an Hispanic woman with two girls, four and seven, I guessed, and a church-pew sister white-knuckling it by the water fountain, probably another preggers.

I made a bee-line to the hazard-orange plastic chair and took a seat. A straight up, sit and wait.

My mind began to drone. Buzz lines knitted my brow.

Why had I succumbed to pity and agreed to be William's heterosexual guinea pig? What a sap I am! All that malarkey about how he wanted to be "sure" he was gay. What do I care? What do I do now?

I studied the two little girls – and their mama. The seven-year-old clambering over the milk-of-magnesia kiddy table was a classic tomboy. Who invented that? It should be tomgirl.

I caught her eye and said, "*¿Quantos anos tienes?*"

"I'm Seven." Lash! Snap! She whipped her pony tail.

"*Siete.*" I said with aplomb.

Insulted, she gave me an exasperated "Seven, *estupida.*"

Undaunted by my chastisement, and aware of my annoying grown-up voice, I threw my hat in the ring once more, asking the back of her keister as she slithered, Anaconda style, down the seventies-style, Avocado-green plastic chair: "What do you want to be when you grow up."

A ponytail exclamation point hung over her butt-plop on the floor, her legs positioned in an upside down Y. She blew, puffing up a straggling bang and retorted emphatically. "A Policeman."

"A Policeman!" I crowed. And then I smiled and added, "You'd be a Police-woman…"

She glared a toofy-mouthed snarl. You'd think I'd stolen her lolly.

"Police-w.o.m.a.n," I spelled out and smiled.

Sussing a truffle of undefinable demotion, she picked up a red plastic dump truck and ran over my foot.

A giggle switched my attention -- stage right -- to dainty sister who slid home-base into the newly vacated chair quick as a toot sweet.

Pleased, Miss Pretty turned over and sat upright scooching her tush to the back. Her hot pink tennis shoes with purple twinkling hearts, blinked as they stood sentry at the lip of the seat. She looked up into my face

"Alrighty then ... What do *you* want to be when *you* grow up."

Gathering muster, Miss Pretty flipped her plaited braids forward in defiance of her sister's watchful glare.

"King. I want to be King."

"King, huh," admiring Miss Pretty's ambition.

Butting in, Tomboy said: "You can't be King, stupid." She struck a policeman pose and shot Miss Pretty between the odious.

"Why not?" Miss Pretty protested.

"You're a girl...stupid. Only *Boys* can be Kings!"

Perhaps "stupid" was Tomboy's only personal descriptive word, but without pause, she mimed slipping a quarter into a slot machine and pulling the handle. Her head rolled in time with the spinning lemon-cherry wheels of dreamy chance. She said: "Ka-Ching, ding-a-ding, ding. Ha!" as if that was her lever of irrefutable logic.

Undaunted, Miss Pretty pouted, and then sprang a sunflower smile of satisfaction and harrumphed, "Queen! Then, I'll be a Queen."

Tomboy glared at me then glimmered a "bad-seed" smile. "You can't be a Queen."

"Why not? I'm a girl, ain't I?"

"You don't have the dresses! Checkmate!"

Miss Pretty and I shared a knowing smile. Dresses were *no problema.*

Mama had been watching. She looked to me and said, "They are their own persons."

As I pursed my lips, thinking, my name was called by Thumbelina eyes. I stood and gave an appraising glance at a woman in a white coat, an open door, and the uncertainty beyond.

At my side, Mama said, "*Si, mucho* work and worry, but *mucho simpatica* satisfaction, and . . . snatches of joy you get no other way."

I turned my eyes back to her.

She cocked her head, arched her brows, and gave me a questioning smile.

"Hmmm." I stepped away with my own bemused smile.

# GHOST WRITERS IN THE RYE
## A parody on Ghost Riders in the Sky
## Philip Shafer

A work-worn hand went writing out,
    one dark and stormy day.
Upon the page she raised her pen,
    and thought about her pay.
When all at once a flood of words,
    in red-eyed rush she saw,
Squirming to life, engulfing her,
    as down a mighty maw.

Yippie Zane Grey.
Yippie L'amour.
Ghost writers in the rye.

The ragged words burst forth from
    fifty frantic scratching hands.
Attached to fifty ghostly forms,
    forced to mandated brands.
The wraiths compelled against deadlines,
    they had to write or die,
A flow of words to tell a tale,
    on just a slug of rye.

Refrain

Their knuckles white, their nails chewed red,
    their faces dripping sweat,
They're writing hard to catch them words,
    but they ain't caught 'em yet.
They cringed as agents cracked the whip,
    exposed without defense.
The phantom words contorting in
    syntax and mood and sense.

Refrain

The writers wrote on by her and
    she heard one call her name,
"You want to save your soul from hell
    writing for others' fame?
Then scribbler change your ways today,
    or with us you will stay,
Trying to catch these devil words,
    Five-thousand more each day."

Refrain

Ghost Riders in the Sky was written in 1948 by Stan Jones.
One reviewer called it "the best song ever written." Zane Grey
and Louis L' Amour wrote over 160 western novels. Neither
worked as a ghost writer, but their prolific work and genre
makes them appropriate heroes. Ghost writers and hacks de-
serve a song.

## LISTENING IN
### Kristine Limont

No, no, you don't understand." My mother's voice was laced with an unfamiliar edge. I felt goose bumps rise under my shirtsleeves. "They did every test there is. They are sure it is some kind of progressive muscle disease, like muscular dystrophy, and one day all three of them will need wheelchairs."

It was a sunny afternoon in early spring two months past my 10th birthday. My mother and her two best friends, Ann and Jeannie, or Mrs. Lemeris and Mrs. Pipes, as I addressed them, were in the dining room where my family had dinner each night. Their voices were low though I heard most of what was said. I knew it was wrong to listen in, but my mother's sobs had me rooted to my spot. I was perched close to the top of the staircase out of sight but within earshot, a short hallway separating me from the first floor room where the women sat. My head rested on one of the banister's wooden legs.

"Dottie," I recognized the voice of Mrs. Pipes. I liked it because there always seemed to be a laugh powering her words, though no laughter lingered today. "There must be something that can be done. What about seeing other specialists?"

"Jean is right." Mrs. Lemeris' voice was tight and clipped. She was a no-nonsense woman I found more than a little scary.

My mom's sobs turned to outright crying, something I had never heard before, and it scared me. I looked over my knees at my feet planted on the next step, winter white against the pale blue carpet. I raised them up and held my legs straight out in the air. I scissor kicked like when I swam in the pool. I rotated my ankles. I lifted my arms overhead and moved them in big backstroke circles.

The adult conversation faded as I worked on this puzzle in my head. I looked across the blue sea of living room carpet out the rectangular windows that bracketed our front door. The earth had thawed and readied itself for new shoots of green grass, crocuses, and daffodils, spring a shy kiss in the air.

*Progressive.* I knew what the word meant, moving forward or getting better or something like that. I couldn't put it together with whatever this bad thing was the adults were so upset about; most of all I saw no way I could be part of it. I thought about marching right into the room where my mom and her friends were, showing them just how all right I was. I could hop on one foot while turning in a circle. I could sit on the floor and jump up. I could do some jumping jacks. But I didn't. I leaned my head back on the banister leg, closed my eyes and listened. I did my best to ignore the somersaults deep in my belly.

The friends began their goodbyes and I went up the stairs to my bedroom. I lay down on the chenille bedspread and turned on the radio hoping to hear Casey Kasem's show and lose myself in a world I knew, a world I understood and felt safe in.

## THE MISTY VEIL
### Millie McCoo

I can't remember when the black veil first descended over my face and hung a shadow between me and the world. I was around 11 or so when I noticed it. In my earlier childhood, there had been a hint, a shadow barely visible. But by this age it had thickened, resembling a fog, a gloomy mist.

It was worse in the mornings. I wouldn't have noticed it so much if my sister Marilyn and I hadn't shared a bedroom, which we did from our pre-teen years until college. Marilyn was only a year and a half older yet we were so different. When she woke up, she would urge me to "get up, get up, it's time to move!" I tried to ignore her by pretending not to hear. Then, singing *con brio*, she'd go down the hall to the bathroom to wash up. I would roll toward the wall and yank my blanket up to my ears to shut out the brutal gaiety.

She'd return to the room accompanied by chatter. "What should I wear? Do you think these socks go with my blouse? Which belt is better, this one or this one? Maybe I'll wear bangs today."

Consciousness came to me slowly through the veil. I was always the last of the four kids to use the bathroom. I struggled to get my clothes on; I was lucky to remember to put on socks, which I always thought so ridiculous, since they would constantly gather at the back of my shoes and bunch down under my heels by the end of the day. My hair was so thick the brush wouldn't reach my scalp. It took fortitude to comb through the nighttime tangles. I had what they called a tender scalp, so it was always unpleasant. My sister would grab my comb and brush and give me a ponytail or a thick braid down my back. We were in the same school and she didn't want her younger sister to be an embarrassment, she often teased me. While I dreaded her early morning liveliness, I longed to learn her secret and wanted to be more like her. She was one of the popular girls at school.

Breakfast for me was an ordeal. The last thing I wanted in the morning was food. I was usually the last at the table. By the time I managed to gag everything down so my mother would release me, the hominy grits had hardened into jagged peaks of grainy cement, and cold grease coated the bacon and scrambled eggs. The orange juice mixed with the lingering mint flavor of the toothpaste from my badly-rinsed mouth. When I left for school it was with a nauseous stomach.

It wasn't until many years later that I associated the appearance of the veil with the arrival of menses. Perhaps it had to do with the hormone deluge that began at age 11, surged throughout my teens, twenties and thirties and continued its chaotic course into my early fifties. For many years, I blamed the start of my chronic unhappiness on boys and my fascination with them, as well as my fear. I was taller than most of them, which didn't help. Cystic acne ravaged my face and worsened throughout my teens despite all the ministrations of my mother and various dermatologists. I felt powerless; I felt I deserved the disfigurement.

But most of the difficulties I had facing life had to do with my shadowy companion. I thought I had a deep personality flaw. My mother used to tell me to "buck up." People I knew, and often strangers, ordered me to "smile!" I had no idea why I heard this so often. Lucky ones, like my sister and the friends I was drawn to, held the secret. They knew how to be happy despite the dark mist, which I assumed enshrouded everyone as it did me. They had a way to dissolve it and their cheeriness and the ease with which they moved through the day all sunshine-y happy was a testament to their strength and a contrast to what I assumed was my lack of willpower and weak character.

This was the 1950's America. Boundless, frenetic joy came at me from all angles. Sheriff John and his Lunch Brigade beamed through the chunky TV tube in black, gray and white. He melodically exhorted his little viewers to "laugh and be happy," to be one of the good girls and boys and "spread cheer." He'd sing: "When you look out the window to a dark and gloomy day, break out a smile and in a while, the gloom will go away." It advised to "get rid of worry in a hurry, chase your blues away, just laugh and be happy all the live…long…day!" I sang it repeatedly to myself. It didn't work.

The Mickey Mouse Club started its run with my age group, whom they dubbed the "Merry Mouseketeers". It's Newsreel segment noted that it was dedicated to "The Leaders of the 21st Century." So much responsibility. I knew I had to chase those blues away if I were to live up to my destiny. I had to smile like Annette and Darlene and Jimmy and Teddy. I had to "just" laugh and be happy.

No matter how hard I tried to chase the blues away, the misty veil would lower unexpectedly, sometimes when I was alone; more often, and denser, when I was around other people. I wrote a poem in my teens about what I called "my good friend." But this friend was an unwelcome companion. I named it loneliness. I wrote that "often when I am in a crowd of people so happy and gay, my friend will tap me on my shoulder and whisper, 'come away, come away.'" It would pull me out of life, back into the mist.

I was in my twenties when I found out about Churchill's black dog, the name he'd given his dark moods, and which affected me as a suffocating veil. I had depression, not a character defect, and I wasn't alone. In my forties, Prozac came on the market and gave me the help I needed to step out of the mist.

# FLYING IN TIBET:
## A VERY SHORT LOVE STORY
### Barb Huntington

I came to Tibet to die. Too recently I had watched parents, husband, and friends lose their dignity, bodies, and minds. Seeing them trapped and dependent on caregivers who, no matter how compassionate, might lose their temper over a third diaper change in the wee hours, I had vowed to stay healthy and fit. Despite yoga, hiking, organic food and daily brain exercises on my iMac, I knew something was broken. I meditated, but enlightenment took the form of cold car keys—the ones I couldn't find in my purse. There was no one else in the house to blame for their inappropriate placement in the refrigerator. After a series of tests, young Dr. Miller confirmed my worst fears, blurting out,

"You know that people with female relatives with Alzheimer's have a greater chance of developing it themselves? Well, your mother…" That is where I stopped listening and began planning my last adventure.

One of the hardest parts of losing your life partner early is not having that comfortable person to bounce your ideas off. A child of the Beatles era, I had looked forward to traveling to

119

our Isle of Wight and bouncing grandchildren on my knee when I was sixty-four. At some point I had begun to hate the Fab Four for their fantasy as I gardened and traveled alone. Life was unfair, but that's life.

The catalog showed high snow-covered peaks and Tibetan prayer flags, but the picture of the Buddhist professor who led the tour was the deciding factor in choosing that company. I told myself it was because I wanted to learn more about Tibetan Buddhism, but Jim was tanned and thin, his gray hair held back in a pony tail, reminiscent of the handsome hippies of my youth. I had been a faithful wife for forty years, but when a lengthy computer search revealed he also was widowed, I let my imagination go. Sometimes when I let my imagination go, it goes too far. No entanglements! It hurts to lose a loved one to death. No, I was doing this alone.

On that first day in Katmandu, our tour group stayed at a Western style hotel. I was at the opposite end of the long table from Jim and noticed we were the only ones who had not been served. Then our meals arrived, lentil soup; of course, everyone else had meat.

That night Jim lectured on the history of Buddhism in Tibet, the immolation of monks, the escape of the Dalai Lama, the bravery of students in the face of Goliath China. He brought up how his student assistant had to negotiate to allow one of our members to come on the trip. She had joined an organization to free Tibet and the Chinese government had originally denied her visa. His laughing deep blue eyes looked directly at me. I didn't know he was even aware of the snag that had almost derailed my plans.

That night, bundled in my down jacket, I sat on the balcony of my hotel room staring at the mountains and remembering an old biography I had read. It was about a Buddhist monk who carried the wisdom and karma of untold generations. In it, Tibetan Masters defied gravity and flew through the crags. Even though the book was eventually proved to be a hoax, and the author a plumber in London, that story had become the basis of my plan. As my thoughts flew, I heard a soft guitar and whistling from the next balcony and recognized a folk song from my youth. I began to sing along.

*In the land of Oden, there stands a mountain,*
*One thousand miles in the air.*
*From edge to edge, this mountain measures*
*One thousand miles square.*
*A little bird comes a wingin',*

*Once every million years,*
*Sharpens his beak,*
*And then he swiftly disappears.*
*Thus when this mountain is worn away,*
*This to eternity will be one single day.*

The whistling changed to a deep gentle male voice, harmonizing with my own. The song over, I crept back to my room under the soft quilt and dreamed of flying.

In the following days I lost my will to stay away from him. Walking at that elevation exhausted me, but I would amble a short distance from camp to meditate and then he would be there to sing, and talk of our gardens and grandchildren and the adventures and misadventures of our youth.

Our last two days were to be at a Buddhist monastery that hung precariously on a cliff. There were many caves around it

121

and I had scouted out one I could reach with my wobbly
knees—one that had a beautiful ledge for my taking off spot.
That night, after singing , I found my way up the cliff.  There
was no doubt about jumping.  Alzheimer's would destroy any
hope of "doing the garden, digging the weeds" from my Beat-
les fantasy. Then a warm arm held me tight.  I had been too
involved in my reverie to hear him come up.  Warm lips in the
Tibetan cold.  Comfort and love.

He asked:

"Jumping?"

I nodded,

"Flying"

"Alzheimer's?"

Another nod.

"Me, too."

Another kiss;

And then.

Holding hands,

We flew.

# LEARNING TO KNIT
# WITH MRS. KNIGHT
## Janet Gastil

I learned to knit at The Bishop's School for Girls in La Jolla. Back in 1949, Bishop's was an Episcopal college preparatory boarding school for girls only. Mama sewed my uniforms. We girls wore dark blue jumpers, white long-sleeved blouses, and classic navy blue blazers. Both my parents were attorneys, but I was still from the poorest family at Bishop's. Most of the girls were polite, but some were rude and snooty. Eyeing my uniform on the first day at Bishop's, one girl said, "Nice rags, off the rack at Montgomery Ward's?" I knew she was envious of my homemade but well-tailored uniforms. I answered her, "Private school, private seamstress." I was proud of my mother's skill and I think that's where I got my love of creating things with yarn and fabrics.

Mrs. Knight, our housemother, was stuck with the job of caring for us 9th grade girls during our unprogrammed hours. That meant she had to keep us out of trouble between "sports" and dinner, between evening study hall and bedtime, Saturday afternoon and evening, and Sunday afternoon—times we often spent in Scripps Hall, our dormitory. At the top of the stairs near the middle of the long hallway of Scripps, we had a "sitting room" where we socialized or had meetings when we were not otherwise busy. We sat on wicker sofas and chairs, or lounged on the large red wool rug with giant flowers. Mrs. Knight often joined us there. She was a knitter. Her specialty was Argyle socks, in the Scottish design with tall diamonds pierced by narrow diagonal stripes of varied colors. We could count on Mrs. Knight for expert tutelage in knitting.

On Friday afternoons, those of us who were caught up on our schoolwork and therefore eligible for a walk into the village could sign up for a faculty chaperone to accompany us into town. Mrs. Knight was the one always eager to visit the yarn store. We knitters liked to go there even if we didn't need more yarn. Mrs. Knight suggested a neck scarf as a first project for me.

Every ninth-grader at Bishop's got a weekly allowance of $1.25, to spend as she chose. It took me three weeks of saving up from my allowance to prepare for my purchase. With two other beginning knitters, and Mrs. Knight as our chaperone, we set out for the village shopping district.

The yarn store beckoned to us from an arcade of small shops in downtown La Jolla, a short walk from Bishop's. Many shelves lined the wall, divided into open boxes, each one filled with a different yarn: wool, cotton, mohair, nylon, silk; thin yarns, thick yarns; yarns in dozens of colors. I selected a skein of nylon yarn in the color of claret wine. I squeezed the warm squishy-soft yarn between my fingers and watched it go back to its original shape when I let go. From a display hanging on an adjacent wall I chose a pair of dark red shiny aluminum knitting needles, size "U.S.8," ten inches long. Purchasing the yarn and needles to knit the scarf I had planned, with the money saved from my allowance, satisfied my desire for a project all my own.

Back in our dormitory sitting room on Saturday afternoon, Mrs. Knight patiently taught me how to cast on 60 stitches. I was a slow learner and sometimes I just wrapped the yarn around the needle without securing it. I practiced the wrap-and-secure process until I had mastered it. I held up the yarn just right, between left fingers and thumb, wove the needle through the loop with my right hand, pulled it off my fingers, and slid it onto the needle in my right hand until, at last, I had cast on 60 perfect, well secured stitches and Mrs. Knight pronounced it ready for the first row of knitting.

Mrs. Knight showed me how to stick the point of the needle I held in my right hand through the closest cast-on loop on the left-hand needle, then wrap the yarn clockwise around the needle and pull the loop off the left needle and onto the right. I messed it up so badly that I had to pull all 60 stitches off and start over, several times. At the end of the afternoon, my project was ready for a second row—and I felt more than ready to put it away forever.

By Sunday afternoon I decided to resume the challenge. After three more rows, it didn't look right. "Both sides are bumpy," I complained to Mrs. Knight. "Something is wrong. Where's the smooth side?"

The ever-patient Mrs. Knight examined my work. "This is how it's supposed to look. It's called 'garter stitch,' and it's the same on both sides. You're doing very well."

"The sweater my grandmother made doesn't look like this. It has one bumpy side and one smooth side, a right side and a wrong side. My knitting has no right side."

"Your sweater has what we knitters call a 'stockinette stitch.' To make that, you knit one row, and then you purl one row. When you knit, you slide each stitch to the back—away from you. When you purl, you slide the stitches off to the front, towards you. When you alternate the knit rows and the purl rows, one side is smooth and the other is what you just called 'bumpy.'"

"So, if I want a scarf that's smooth on one side, like my sweater, I have to learn two different stitches."

"That's right. And learning the second one will be easier. It's best if you just knit your first piece and get used to the knit stitch. Your scarf will be the same on both sides, very nice looking and warm too. Then I'll teach you the purl stitch, for your next piece. Okay?"

"Okay," I said. I felt small and meek. Some of the girls were knitting Argyles, while I just concentrated on knitting the next row of my plain scarf. I felt the same as I did years ago when Mama taught me how to add numbers: she said I had to get the whole page of addition problems done quickly and perfectly before she taught me subtraction.

My knit stitches marched on, row after row, through the sharp clear days of October and our field hockey season. A twinge of excitement grew as the strands of dark red nylon yarn turned into a vibrant band of fabric that I could stretch out on my desk and then squeeze back into a soft ball in my hands.

126

As the weeks rolled off the calendar I felt less awkward. My scarf was half done. I kept saving my allowance each week, so that I could buy more yarn for my next project. By the cooler days of November I had learned to knit faster. The errors and unravelings grew fewer. The exciting anticipation grew as the threads on the needles yielded my vibrantly colored scarf. During the cloudier, darker days of December, I declared the scarf long enough. Mrs. Knight showed me how to bind off my finished work, by pulling each stitch over the one ahead of it, until no stitches were left on the needle.

My parents came to take me back home to Alpine, for the Christmas holiday. I said to Mama, "I love you, Mama. Thank you for being my mother." I wrapped the finished red scarf around her neck.

## SWIMMING COACH
### Millie McCoo

I can decide which Millie I will be this moment.
The dark one, depressed and in dread
Or the light, blissful, enchanted one.
If, as so often happens in the morning,
I awake in misery,
Aswirl in the fathomless pool of sadness into which, unbidden,
I have plunged overnight.
I can remind myself that I know how to swim.
I have stores of fat that make me buoyant,
I can float upwards from the blue-black into the blue-green
Into the sunlit shallows,
Burst into the air
And take in the breath of freedom from the undertow of sadness.
I am more than a helpless neurotic, drowning in despair:
I can watch the miserable adolescent, looking to others for acceptance, drift by,
Float past the nervous adult, mistrustful of her own wisdom.
I reach for the child inside of me.
Remembering the stroke is like riding a bicycle

Muscle memory.

I can choose to be the spirited one, welcoming all the promises of the day.

## MORNING
### Kristine Limont

Through the window I see you perched, the sleek profile of your back. Graceful crisp lines frame jet-black feathers, all neat and squared away; you're no swallow in a frumpy housecoat. I stare out my window screen, the tiny geometric beginning of your tableau. The vertical fence posts are topped by crisscrossed lattice, topped with a horizontal four by four, topped by you. The neighboring roof, a canvas that further locks you into a grid of shingles and rectangular chimney lines. Chirp. I chirp back, which sets your head twisting side to side. Chirp. In response to my excited chirps you salute with your left wing and bob your head under for a quick peek, before the dark side shuts. I sing; you salute. We go through several rounds until I become convinced we're conversing and let out a long trill of chatter. You fly away revealing fluffy white tuft of chest and underbelly. I guess we are done talking.

## MIDNIGHT MOMS
### Philip Shafer

**M**adeline circled the block humming, trying to recall the words beyond *"M'appari."* Just thirty minutes earlier she'd thrilled with a girlish flutter. More than shake hands and say, "What a magnificent gala," Luciano Pavarotti lingered several minutes visiting and, she felt certain, lusting for her with undisguised enthusiasm.

Now the dark streets were quiet. Stimulated emotions and thoughts washed freely to the surface of her mind. Lovers eased the urgent desire. The lonely ache of widowhood lingered undimmed after four years. The fulfilling satisfaction of shared purpose, shared joy, shared disappointment, shared anticipation, shared life, throbbed dull, but persistent, by its absence. The unfocused need of motherhood called softly poignant.

Madeline saw no cruising cars, no loitering clump of men. She parked and with a twinge of apprehension mounted the porch to the once grand house. The key she'd been given opened the front door and she immediately saw the house had been compartmentalized. She unlocked the second door on the right and stepped into a small studio.

"It's Mrs. Anderson."

Her soft announcement got no response. Gloria slept in the narrow bed. The infant slept in a plastic laundry basket atop a packing crate. Madeline made a quick survey of diapers, clean shirts and night gown, formula. She checked the time, listened for sounds of stirring, and then quietly washed the few dishes. An eight ounce bottle warm, she waited for the tiny voice.

Exchanging anticipatory coos through diaper changing, the ten-week-old girl soon sucked hungrily cradled in Madeline's left arm.

The report said "colicky." With infant upright after each two ounces Madeline patted and stroked, rocked and walked until she got a burp. Seven ounces down the girl slept, limp as a rag. Madeline lowered her gently to her bassinet feeling the break of separation.

Home by two, Madeline mused. Would pressing flesh with the famous tenor give that kind of feeling?

\* \* \*

Robert circled the block, his eyes darting right and left. He studied the few pedestrians for revealing signals, reaching for keys, glancing about, but pace and purpose locked on a specific vehicle, the sign of a potential parking space. Robert drove while amused curiosity rippled through his mind.

Madeline? It was twelve years ago, my third year of law school, one of Mom's charity events, a social obligation for me. She admonished me. "You're to be charming, polite, and attentive to the wives and widows, especially the widows." She smiled and elaborated. "The committee members with attractive daughters bring them to entice the bachelors and husbands." Laughing out loud, Mom said, "Young flesh works even better than champagne to boost contributions." I met both Madeline and Linda at that event. Madeline came as a wife, but she was my age. She made a generous contribution and then hired me to draw up legal papers.

She laughed, the same open laugh my mom used to admit her fundraising ploys. "If I wait 'til you pass your bar exams you'll charge more, be constrained by fear of being disbarred, and won't have that drive to prove yourself."

Madeline wanted to open a business of her own but hide it from her rich husband who wouldn't approve. Our secret business affair succeeded and flourished. Our secret personal affair flamed passionately brief. Madeline said, "I love my husband. I'm very loyal to him, in my way." We remained friends. Linda? Linda was love. Fulfillment, purpose, joy. Linda was . . .

"There!" Robert hit the brakes, reversed for half a block, and captured the parking space.

Madeline noticed him enter and take a seat at the back of the meeting room. The speaker from County Welfare, emphasized for the third time: "There is nothing so needed, nothing so quickly used up, nothing whose lack is so devastating, as a mother's sleep. Mrs. Anderson's Midnight Moms is doing more in its simple direct way than millions of dollars of taxpayer funding. Sign up. Help save a mother and her baby."

The gushing compliments, the serious questions, ran twenty minutes before she could say: "Robert?"

"Hello, Madeline. My mother said you asked about me." His doubting smile preceded the question. "Legal advice?"

"Come on. Let's get a coffee. Anderson manufacturing doesn't have an in-house attorney. The firm we use is outrageously expensive, pompous, and too cautious. And ... I never told you how sorry I felt."

"You were in Haiti, then Paris, with your own tragedy. Linda said, 'We're out of milk. I'll be ten minutes.' She was struck by a swerving truck and died instantly. I had to get out of LA. It took a while. I had my girls. Mom, and Linda's parents, kept pestering me to bring them home.

"Lindsey's eight, Jean is ten. So, I'm back, with my own firm. Yeah. Spoiled trust-fund-kid playing at lawyering. It's working. Does Midnight Moms need an attorney?"

Madeline searched Robert's face. "You heard the social worker's description. We have two kinds of volunteers: empty nest moms with experience, time, no grandchildren yet and who want to recapture the joy of holding a baby; and ... women like me." Madeline laughed. ". . . women who can sleep 'til noon if we want."

Robert tipped his head in understanding.

"We don't send them to dangerous neighborhoods or unstable households, but they, more often their husbands, worry about liability. My organization is incorporated, but I don't want it destroyed by some law suit either. We need 'memos of understanding' waiver forms, something like that. Will you help?"

They stared at each other, aware of the gap in their lives.

Madeline said: "Bring your girls. They can play in my extravagantly heated pool while we discuss possibilities."

## PROKOFIEV AND REMEMBRANCE
### Janet Gastil

I'm onstage too late for one more practice of those zippy sixteenth notes with dozens of accidentals. It's June ninth, 2015. I sit directly behind our concertmaster, easily visible from anywhere in our full house. In five minutes we'll be playing Sergei Prokofiev's Fifth Symphony.

I put down my violin and look around. My friend Eve Gerstle sits in the front row, elegantly dressed and alert. She comes to every concert we play. She sees me, smiles, and waves her hand. She's one hundred-and-one years old. Prokofiev composed this Symphony in 1944, while World War II devastated his country and slaughtered his fellow Russians--1944 while Eve suffered in a concentration camp in Germany. She lost her parents, her husband, her aunts, uncles and cousins. She was the only survivor.

I've never played through this Fifth Symphony without a few mistakes.I look back at Eve, and take courage. I promise myself that today I will play for her, the best I can.

In 1944, I was seven years old; I began music lessons and held a violin in my hand for the first time. My father worked at the Davis Monthan Air Force Base in Tucson. He brought the crew of a B29 bomber home to us and two of their wives came to live with us in a federal housing project. That B29 crew flew to the South Pacific. Their plane was shot down. They were all killed. I cried, bewildered by my first experience of untimely, unjust death—my first grief.

Our conductor steps to the podium amid polite applause. He raises both arms, his baton poised for an instant, and he sets the tempo. The wind instruments begin the strong, dark opening. We violins take over the theme, and the symphony is launched. The music of Prokofiev envelops us and our audience.

I know the trouble spots. I feel the excitement of the symphony. My friend Sarah and I share a music stand. She'll notice every missed nuance, just as I will hear the mistakes of others. We are friends. We cheer for each other just as our audience cheers us—an accolade we earn by playing our best. The performance is a blend of them and us.

We finish the last and most challenging movement of "Prokofiev's Fifth." Our conductor's arms sweep up, calling us to stand and bow. Our audience applauds. They leave the hall slowly, moved by great music. We pack up our instruments and head for home.

Getting into my car I realize that I got almost every note, every nuance I struggled for all those weeks of rehearsal. Sarah never had to suppress a gasp. Eve never saw my bow go the wrong way. I swell with a sense of accomplishment.

Driving home, I think again of 1944, the year Sergei Prokofiev composed this fabulous music, near Moscow, in the safety of a camp set up for Russian artists and musicians. He wrote music while 20 million of his countrymen perished. What was he thinking as he composed this tempestuous symphony? What was Eve thinking tonight as she listened to that music penned in 1944, as her family perished? Did we play themes and express ideas that only Prokofiev, Eve, and those who lived there at that time can appreciate?

## WHAT WE SEE
### Barb Huntington

**We** walk in the wild forest, you and I.

**Do** you see the houses and factories ready for our shaping,

**Not** a wasted branch or stone?

**See** our supremacy in the soaring skyscrapers,

**Things** that fly or move us through the land?

**As** primitive genes bend to our reshaping

**They** define our power.

**Are** other worlds trembling at our might?

143

**We** ride among our achievements, you and I.

**See** how we have fashioned machines to do our thinking,

**Things** to pump blood, and furnish oxygen through our bodies

**As** we rush to replace flesh unsuitable for skies of pesticide and radiation?

**We** are the masters of our world!

**Are** other worlds trembling at our might?


*An acronistic poem

# ON THE WAY TO JAIPUR
## Laura Bottaro Costner

Aashi sat beside a tall table as her father, Kemlesh, ironed laundry inches from the street. At both sides of the table were piles of used brick that would pass for rubble were they not in the ancient town of Neemrana in the heart of Rajasthan. In India work takes place wherever there is space. Across the street a barber set up shop in a canopied stall. It would be hard to miss the man whose face was covered with shaving cream and the barber rinsing his blade in a pan of water. Two other men sat with them presumably catching up on the news or gossip. This all seemed quite natural to Aashi, the 11 year old girl, as natural as the monkeys running up the trees and jumping from one limb to another. As natural as her father carrying on the family business on the street while his shop was being rebuilt.

The ironing table was covered with a blanket and a white sheet. There was no electric cord coming out of the oversized iron because the heat was generated by hot coals. In the corner sat a water bottle and a cell phone. While he kept his eyes on the shirt he was ironing, Aashi was free to look about. Located on the highway between Delhi and Jaipur, the town of

8,000, ninety-eight per cent of whom are Hindu, sees a fair share of tourists who find it a convenient lunch stop. She looked down the street and there they were.

A group of 20 Europeans or Americans had just disembarked from a coach. She guessed they were Americans by the sheer zeal they exhibited in taking pictures as soon as they arrived. Their overall manner was relaxed; they were far from somber like some groups. No doubt this was the first country town that they had visited after landing in Delhi 3 or 4 days before. The traffic on the narrow street through the town's center stopped them in their tracks. It was a steady stream of motor scooters, cars, motorized rickshaws, bicycles, tractors, trucks and, here and there, a cow or a camel. The curbs and sidewalks of urban India don't exist in Neemrana and neither do traffic lights or road markings like lines. Everyone to some degree drives on the left side and passes whatever is in front of them if there is even a few inches of leeway. It looked like their Indian tour guide was giving them instructions on where to walk and where they would cross. They looked at him with raised eyebrows as he pointed to the dirt drop-off that would be their path. Fear struck when a couple of motor scooters careened by with beeping horns. The piercing sound seemed to never stop because there were almost as many scooters as people in the town. Aashi wondered if the guide told them to watch out for the open trenches and roadwork that never ends.

As they ambled down the street she observed that they all looked pretty much alike with their muted colors, short hair and hats, some straw, some floppy. She was dressed in a bright purple and pink tunic with turmeric colored pants that were gathered at the ankle. All the women she knew wore vibrant colors and a multitude of patterns which made it nearly impossible to find two saris or tunics that looked alike. To her, all of the Americans with the exception of two women, were dressed like her father, pants and a shirt. She thought it was strange that all these women dressed like men. She had seen young Indian girls in jeans in Delhi and on TV but they were few and far between in the towns and villages in the country-side.

She watched as they approached the street market. Flatbed carts and dark blue plastic milk cartons stacked in twos were topped with shallow bowls measuring about two feet across. Each one was filled with a mound of produce. They began snapping pictures of fruits and vegetables usually with one of them posed in front of the display. She had seen this before and decided this time to ask, "Papa, don't they have fruits and vegetables in America?" Kemlesh assured her that America has plenty of produce. He told her that tourists always go for the colors. "Our carrots are more red than orange, the chili peppers are red and orange and the colors of spices really catch their eye." He also pointed out that most Americans shop in big stores so they find street markets a novelty. It made her smile to see how happy they were as they found different angles from which to snap pictures of food. "Do we have big food stores in Delhi and Mumbai?" Kemlesh continued to iron while explaining, "Yes, but most people still prefer open markets and small shops because they are convenient to get to and the food is fresher."

Mixed in between vegetable stalls was a canopied stand selling Indian chai. She had seen in the past that hardly any tourists try it. Maybe this time would be different because the tour guide and the coach driver each bought a glass. She could tell they were trying to convince some of the group to forget what they had read in their tour books about avoiding street food. "Come on, give it a try," said the guide holding up his glass. They smiled but as usual there were no takers. All of a sudden she saw two men laughing and shaking their heads up and down. They stepped forward, and within seconds, each had a glass of the milky tea in his hand. Everyone, including the tea brewers, laughed as the men toasted each other and took a large swig. Aashi laughed along with them and blurted out, "If I went to America, I would try new things."

Some of the tourists looked around in all directions while waiting for the tea break to finish. That's when someone spotted Aashi and Kemlesh. Five or six people waved at Aashi. Their smiles were contagious and they seemed so happy that she waved back. Next some of them started to snap pictures. Her father kept his eyes on his work but Aashi eyes lit up and she continued waving. As others joined in she was sure every tourist had a picture of her and her father to take home. Suddenly a tractor pulling a 4-wheel cart drove by. Eight women in bright colored saris were seated in the cart and, like a school of fish, the pointed fingers and cameras changed direction. For the Americans it was a sight to behold. A government program offers farmers a subsidy to purchase tractors. Most are used in the fields but many, like the one passing by, are used to pull carts or simply as personal transportation.

About 10 minutes later the group moved on and Aashi assumed they would soon cross the street and head up the hill to the 15$^{th}$ century Palace, now a restored heritage hotel. Aside from a lunch buffet of curried cuisine, the palace offered visitors the art and architecture of medieval India and spectacular views of the valley. Crossing the street involved the guide walking into the traffic and signaling all moving objects to stop while at the same time hollering at his charges to "hurry up and cross." Most did and within a short time they were exploring the residential area below the palace. The sandstone beige and white houses ranged from small to sizeable. Most had bright turquoise or reddish-orange doors. Fenced-in yards held cows, motor scooters, a car, and sometimes, a garden. One woman was not at all shy about asking locals to take a picture with her. Like the rest of the group, her command of the Hindi language consisted of one word "Nameste." Each time she said the magic word, she put her hands together in a prayerful pose, bowed her head and offered up a smile. They always said yes.

Aashi continued to watch the group navigate the crossing. She looked to see if there were any who hadn't crossed. That's when she spotted the stragglers, a couple, the only couple under forty, and two other women. All were totally captivated by the monkeys swinging on the branches. The street was lined with trees so there was no end to the entertainment above their heads. A few minutes later she heard a loud shriek as the young woman fell in a trench. Her husband jumped in and helped her to her feet. With her arms flailing about she began to shout at one of the other two women. By their gestures, onlookers could tell she was yelling "You pushed me" while the response, just as obvious, was, "I did not." The traffic didn't stop but everything else did. Even Kemlesh put down his iron and watched. In minutes the guide appeared and his cell phone quickly went up to his ear. Soon a car arrived and the woman and her husband, accompanied by the guide, were off to the local hospital for x-rays but not before he helped the other two women across the street and told them to catch up with the group. Aashi wondered why the only couple her parents' age found themselves in the ditch. All the others in the group were her grandparents' age. Her Hindu wisdom led her to one conclusion, 'Bad Karma.' There is no way she could have known that the thirty-something woman had told half of the group to their face, "You're just a bunch of 'old people'."

Since senior sightseers tend to take their time to look about and seldom break any records walking uphill, the two rattled women were able to join the group in time for their midday fix of curried vegetables—eggplant, chickpeas, lentils, and cauliflower all scooped up with roti or, for this group, fork and spoon. The young couple? No injuries except to the woman's pride which made her even more disagreeable. A few days later the tour company hired a car and driver for the couple. Hotels were notified that they were to be assigned rooms far from the group. When they were spotted at the different sights along the way, the woman almost always had her nose in a book. The group's unspoken wish was that their driver spoke 90 percent Hindi and 10 percent English.

## ST. PIERRE AND THE SEA
### Philip Shafer

L ike this, Maddy." My earliest memory, my sister Margaret calling me. I was four, probably. She shinnied out and then dropped down.

St. Pierre was officially described as rocky, barren and foggy. But the sea around our tiny island teemed with life. Seals and thousands of birds crowded the shore. With the added centuries of human habitation, there was a certain accretion of spoil. A few wives produced pitiful herb gardens; a bushy heather grew in a few places; and a single tree grew near the wharf at the end of the street. It and a thicket conspired, huddled close, clinging to and nurturing their precious patch of soil.

I watched her scooting out the limb. I climbed that tree as well as she, but this was new. Her arms wrapped tight, she swung beneath, then dangled and dropped out of sight. Crawling from the dank labyrinth, she brushed her skirts back into place. "See. But don't worry. If you slip, the brush will break your fall." It worked the way she said it would, except my dress, a hand-me-down, Mag's pinafore, remained, caught on spiny branches. Scrambling out, still fully clad, my pullover and woolen socks meeting bloomers above my knees, laughing exultantly at my accomplishment, I sought from Mag, a compliment. A startled look, she searched about. Madame Lecomte stood watching us, her thin lips in a knowing smile. Sad resignation on her face, my sister's gaze returned to me, my underwear proclaiming clear my family's frugality. The soft, warm, strong absorbent cloth emblazoned with the snatches of colored typeface signaled boldly the well-known words: *Fleur de Farine. Marchand de Farine - Le Havre.*

We were genteel poor, Margaret and I. We had a normal childhood for the times, I suppose. In 1925, the year Margaret was born, the Moelleux family moved from Toulouse to Paris as our father, Theodore, progressed up the ladder of bureaucracy in the French Foreign Service. I was born in 1927, and in 1929 Papa was appointed Governor of St. Pierre-Miquelon. It was partly a reward for his war service, partly to get rid of him, and partly to cater to the island's residents who wanted their governor to have some ethnic identification with them. They were ninety percent Norman and Basque. Papa's grandparents were Norman and Basque.

The post was not highly sought. Such jobs were usually held by mediocre men of independent means. The pay was meager, a stipend, plus an added salary based on population. The two islands had forty-six-hundred people. The Moelleux family was poor, with the added burden of maintaining a respectable public image. The one plus was no social competitors with whom we had to keep up. Papa was allotted one assistant. He split the allowance so he had a half-time secretary and Mama had a half-time housekeeper. It gave two island families welcome cash-money income.

The short summers were cool and foggy. The eight months of winter were cold with rain, sleet, snow, high winds, and fog. The Gulf Stream kept the islands ice-free year-around. The economy was cod fishing, with salting, drying, and canning, the tiny and only significant industry. One family bred Silver Fox; several traded in sealskins, but the greatest boon had been "bootlegging" during the American and Canadian Prohibition era. High Canadian imports on cigarettes and spirits remained an incentive to alternative commercial activities. Margaret and I went to school with the island children, made friends with them, played with them, and even participated in social functions with them, but we were outsiders and we were the governor's daughters. Acceptance took years; aloofness lingered.

I was six when I went to sea, my first time on a fishing yawl. In April and October great activity came to our island. Boats gathered from Europe, mostly Bretons and Basque. We had reunions and celebrations, blessings and preparations. St. Pierre overflowed with color and excitement, the babble of languages and talk of fish, the almighty cod, and tales, too, of life at sea, and death. Awesome dangers, awesome beauty, strange mysteries. I never went out on the banks to help them fish; boats would be gone for many weeks. My first trip lasted just two hours while a new ring jig was tested. Duprés, our island's boatwright, watched me as I watched the men working.

"You run and ask the gov'nor if it's all right."

153

I loved it. Hoist and heave, tackle and sheave, mainsail and jib, dozens of lines, masts and spars, planking and keel, the wonderful feel of nautical speed, four knots but a rush of crashing spray, spanker snapped tight, five and the deck at a heel.

Soon, I was invited out again. "A natural sailor," Duprés said. I never got sick. I learned all the terms and most of the warnings. "Red sky at night, mariner's delight," sky and swell, cross chop and soundings, set and drift, current and tide, the responsive quiver of tiller in hand, the visceral blend of boat, sea, and wind.

The chart showed my name, *Iles de la Madeleine.* "Two hundred twenty sea miles through the Cabot Straight. West-northwest by west," Duprés said. "A tough beat up against the wind." He laughed. "But a fair scoot and quick back home." I longed to go there. "Now, Sydney or Glace Bay is another thing. West-southwest and fifty closer."

Our only ferry service came monthly from Sydney on Cape Breton Island, which was hardly an island, being connected by highway and railroad bridges to the rest of Nova Scotia and the whole North American continent. Other service was by special arrangement. Ocean-going ships stopped offshore. People and small cargo came and went by motor launch. That's what we did when we went to France on vacation. Lots of world traffic passed by, sometimes in sight, but we were still isolated.

On a clear day you could see across the water to Lamaline, but it was as isolated as we, out on the end of the Burin Peninsula on Newfoundland, an island itself. St. John's, the nearest big port, was north around Cape Race two hundred sea miles. Halifax was twice as far to the southwest. I never got to either one, but I did get to Cape Breton twice. The first time was a thrilling, desperate day.

Mama became very ill. The motor launch was in for repairs; the ferry wasn't due for a week; and the nearest ship or other power boat couldn't get to St. Pierre for at least a day and a half. Duprés said. "We can do it. Glass is starting back up, fresh breeze northwest, following sea. The Marie France is back in the water, paint bright, new rigging, clean bottom, tight." All the men were fishing at sea. Papa had gone to Quebec for a conference; Margaret didn't like boats and always got sick. I went to help crew and comfort Mama.

Rush to the dock, hurriedly load blankets and food, hurried instructions from the doctor. We were underway in less than an hour, Duprés and Mama, Jacques-Louis and me. It never occurred to us to ask some wife or one of the older children. A misty rain most of the day had stopped but all was drippy wet. Mama gave me a weak, wan smile, but I knew she was terrified. The doctor gave Mama a shot of morphine before we sailed off. He gave me more blue pills for her. "But not before midnight," he said, "and then two more at six o'clock."

Murky gray sky, low scudding clouds, brought pitch-dark night by four. The dark hump of Miquelon to starboard, passed as we moved in fits and starts over flat rippled water to searching gusts. Duprés had warned me but, I was caught unprepared. We came out of the lee to a shrieking blast. Mama moaned as she pitched from her bunk. Lurching, I caught and held her tight, my feet braced on the larboard strakes. The Marie France rolled on her side and seemed content to stay that way. Finally, Jacques-Louis came below to check on me, and calling out, "A stronger blow than we had thought."

Seeing my awkward position and Mama's pale distress, he took Mama from me, calling, "My fault. We left in such a rush, I forgot. There. Get the rails from below. Right. Now these straps. See. Yes. Careful. Not too tight. Is that all right, Madame Moelleux?" He touched her cheek, and then gave me a grin. "Maddy, here, is a good sailor and she'll be a good nurse for you."

We both watched Mama's lips open and close as her head rolled to the side. "Are you all right, girl? Remember, always one hand, a good grip on something solid, and move with the roll."

He went on forward and opened the hatch for a peek in the fore-hold. Coming back searching for leaks, he lifted a plate and checked the bilge."Barely damp so far."

Addressing me directly, he said. "We'll need your help a bit later. Stay here with your mama for now. I think she'll sleep. So rest yourself, but bundle up well before you venture out on deck."

By eight, that first initial shriek had settled to a steady hum. The boat was in a strange corkscrew, the most violence I'd seen so far in my so brief experience, but regular. I must have dozed off for a bit. Jacques-Louis woke me with a nudge and a hot mug. I ate, or rather drank the brew, hot water with a spoonful of brown sugar and one of oatmeal, still softening. I watched him fix his own *gruau* as he stood braced at the swinging stove. He touched Mama and then he said, "Come. Now you're part of my fine crew; it's time you earned your helmsman stripes."

156

No rain but constant splashing spray came stinging cold on my hot face. We three, an island of humanity, close tight, in binnacle's soft glowing light. The vital sea, a different life, churning dark but not enemy. We had to shout, "Eight knots. I have no doubt." The men nodded in agreement.

Duprés called out. "Maddy, *jeune fille*, listen to me. You've not the weight; you'll blow away. So lock your knees beneath that thwart, your arm around the tiller, so. The other here, and hang on, dear." He laughed. "The wind's abeam, sea's quartering, just feel the heave and heel, but don't come up too close. The mainsail's flutter is your clue.

They watched me, coaching, for an hour. I felt it, sure, before they knew it. This boat and me, an entity. I could do it.

"Now take a break, check your mama. Next time's for real."

I dozed some more. At eleven, Mama cried out and thrashed about. She took a sip and held my hand. We listened to the sighing wind, the noises of creaking timbers, the crashing waves, slap and shudder, incessantly. With pitch and roll we swayed, tensing, our dumb response, unceasingly. Her agitation grew intense. I gave my mama two blue pills.

At midnight Duprés had to rest. I took my trick and did my best. Twice, Jacques-Louis was out of sight. Forward, a fairlead broke, again, a slack jib line.

Alone, I crouched in my sou'wester, slicker coat, and pants. Returned, he said, "We're kin, you know. Your mother's great aunt married my father's great uncle. Our family name's Cruzon." I didn't know but thought, Cruzon? Mama helped the wife, Marie, and her two small children. I smiled and shrugged. He laughed, and then we said no more.

The long night passed. It seemed like days. Two hours of sleep, then up again to steer the course or just be there so they could take their nap below. At five, stars broke the overcast, whitecaps faint pale in inky black. The wind now less than twenty knots had veered due north; the waves, taller, were not as steep. At nearly eight the sky grew light. I took the helm while the men raised the mizzen sail. Heave to the wind to ease the strain, break back before we lose headway. More *gruau* plus biscuits and tea, Mama awake, we talked briefly. She took two pills, only two left. A rosy dawn, I slept 'til noon. Apples, hot punch, and more biscuits.

"A beautiful day." High scattered clouds, raw windy cold, two miles of visibility. Yes, beautiful for November. At one o'clock, we saw the radio tower at Dominion and by two-thirty we were dockside there. Seventeen kilometers over the hill to the hospital at Sydney, just half an hour. They were expecting us but still were surprised. We crossed in twenty-two hours and twenty-two minutes, averaging six-and-a-half knots.

I don't know what Duprés and Jacques-Louis did for a week. I rode in the ambulance with Mama and stayed with the doctor's family until Papa came. That's when I started to learn English, and that's when I learned how poor we were. Papa let me return on the Marie France. Mama survived her surgery. I was relieved and secretly pleased to sail home on the Marie France. I said, "Papa will pay you for the trip." I had no idea how much that was, but felt, at least the ferry's fee.

"Oh, no. I don't think so," they said. "We had to test the Marie France and, anyway, there are many ways to repay or help a friend."

We didn't hurry and took note of the weather. We sailed north to Ingonish and anchored in the bay. A boat rowed out to us. We gave them some boxes and they gave us some boxes and a canvas purse. We all slept that night and started home in the morning.

All day, all night. I took my turns and learned to cook at gimbaled stove. They smoked their pipes. We took our naps. The watches passed; the wind had backed. At ten o'clock, our home in sight, the 'English' boat gave us a hail. "It's the revenue inspector's cruiser out of Placentia Bay. If the man asks, just say hello and give your name."

I was just eight but knew the game. My sister Margaret had explained. "They're all smugglers; they all do it." The other boat, a gun on deck, quite politely came in our lee, and paced along matching our speed. The uniformed officer spoke French perfectly. "Good day, Duprés. You're out again?" He cocked his head. "Where have you been?"

"Cape Breton, Dominion, Sydney . . . and we sailed from Ingonish yesterday morning. We needed to tack up to get a good reach home."

Surprised at open honesty, the officer hesitated. My squeaky voice surprised me too as I called out, "Good day, good sir. My name is Madeleine Moelleux. I'm daughter of the governor. We just took my poor mama to Sydney for an emergency operation. We were worried, but now we think she might get well."

The officer smiled, shook his head, and as the cruiser pulled away, raised his hand in friendly salute.

At dock and secure, I bundled up my gear with Mama's blankets and carried it ashore. Our house was two-hundred meters. I could tote the bundle, but looking around for a dolly cart, I realized Duprés and Jacques-Louis were still below. I didn't call but crept softly to the hatch. I watched the men dump the contents of the canvas purse on the bunk, bank notes, dozens of Canadian silver dollars and other coins.

They sensed my presence and turned their heads. Jacques-Louis looked surprised, but Duprés grinned. "Aha! Maddy."

My voice not squeaking at all, I said, "How much is a helmsman's share?"

They stared and then they laughed. Duprés and I and Jacques-Louis had a final hot punch toasting a successful trip. My mug had a taste of rum.

Five months later, catastrophe! Four boats were lost, that was for sure, and one was still long overdue. Just past midday, a clear Monday, the shout rang out, "The Marie France is coming in!" The men and children ran to see. At *Colline d'est* with his spyglass, Duprés studied the distant craft. "It's her all right. She's been bashed in."

Three of the men ran on ahead. The rest of us walked slowly back.

Waiting at dock, the women knew rushing about had no effect on the hard course of destiny. Missing three weeks, the Marie France, without its mast, port side planking ripped clean away, with a pathetic scrap of sail raised on a valiant, broken spar, now in tow by the motor launch, was brought to home.

And on its deck, the entire crew, three men only, two lost at sea. Families in the tiny crowd watched silently, acknowledgment, nervous release, detached despair.

Marie Cruzon, a child at knee, and babe in arms, stared blankly off, beyond the sea's far horizon.

And still I loved to go to sea, but never saw my *Iles Madeleine*

## ABOUT THE AUTHORS

**LAURA BOTTARO COSTNER** is a non-fiction writer who has come to enjoy the freedom of creative nonfiction. What began with memoir writing slowly moved to storytelling and imagined characters. A former teacher and certified financial planner, her previous publications include: Women's Forum, quarterly financial newsletter; Wall Street PDX, monthly Investment Advisor newsletter; Destination: Your Chosen Dreams, article, Successful Money Management Seminars. She has edited numerous manuscripts and publishes Amazon book reviews as Laura Bottaro. Laura lives in San Diego with her husband John and cat, Katie. She is a lifetime fan of British murder mysteries and, for that matter, all things British. She can be reached at laurabottarocostner@gmail.com.

**JANET GASTIL** Writing intrigues me. I love words—old and new. A single word can conjure up hundreds of images. String words together for millions of stories. My academic background taunts me. BA in music, Masters in Poetry, and Doctoral Studies in Linguistics. My husband Gordon and I wrote an historical novel, *Follow the Sun.* It won the San Diego Book Awards for best historical fiction in 2006. The plot was brilliant. The history and anthropology of ancient cultures was illuminating and fascinating—all Gordon's. My "flowing narrative" was mediocre. I still struggle. Current project is a blend of family, San Diego history, politics, and Quaker philosophy.

**EDDY CONRAD HEUBACH** is a native San Diegan, an alumnus of SDSU and a retired SDUSD teacher. He lives in La Mesa. Most of his stories occur in and around southern California. squelchecho@cox.net.

**BARBARA WEEKS HUNTINGTON,** a mother of four grown children and seven grandchildren, has been a civil rights worker, a teacher, CEO of a computer mail order house, technical writer and marketing consultant. She retired from SDSU after 20 years as Director of Pre-professional Health Advising. She holds a BS from SDSU and an MBA from UCLA. She lives in Chula Vista with her dog, Tashi, an organic vegetable garden, and a labyrinth of rocks and succulents. She has published several poems in San Diego anthologies and will soon complete her memoir—Laughing just to Keep from Crying . . . and Rattlesnakes! She posts poetry, memoir, and miscellaneous writings on her blog at https://barbarahuntington.com.

**KRISTINE LIMONT** grew up in the small town of Scituate, MA, the second youngest of five children. TV was limited but books and library nights were limitless, giving her a lifelong love of books. She moved to California when she was twenty. She received a BA from the Monterey Institute of International Studies in 1987. She and her husband were graciously invited to co-parent her single cousin's two children. They are both grown and she just welcomed her third grandchild into this crazy world. In 2013 she took a writing class and later became a member of the INGLY Writers.

**MILLIE MCCOO** wrote her first poem when she was 8 years old. During her school and college years she wrote poetry, plays and satire, some of which were produced and published. As a young adult, she lived in Zambia and Kenya, where she was a freelance writer and radio producer. There followed a 28 year career as a diplomat in the US Foreign Service. She lived and worked in the Middle East, Sub-Saharan Africa and the Caribbean. Now retired Millie is working on a memoir and indulges in her love of poetry, travel and animals.

**PHILIP SHAFER** was born in Ohio and raised in La Jolla, California. His diverse career includes naval officer, commercial helicopter pilot, history teacher, planning consultant, campaign manager, government bureaucrat, and corporate officer. Of curious interest, Shafer is a California certified smoke reader, and for several years wrote the crossword puzzle for a newspaper. After a history and a book on seismic safety, Philip Shafer has published nine romance-thriller novels. Three of those have been San Diego Book Awards Finalists. A fourth, **Shepherd's Secrets**, won their award for best romance novel in 2012. Philip has traveled widely in the Far East and extensively in France. He lives in the beach community of San Diego. He can be found online as authorphilipshafer.

**KAREN SIMONS,** a former librarian and public school educator is a writer of memories, of her own and of others. An alumna of San Diego State University, she came to writing through the OLLI program for adult learners. Her curiosity about how her own life intersects with those of others through geographic and historic grids, informs the pieces she writes. Karensimons675@gmail.com.

**KARY LYNN VAIL,** a native San Diegan, Hollywood expatriate, performance artist, actress, comedian and voyager, is an inspired INGLY newcomer. Autodidactic, storyteller and squirrel of colloquialisms "go whistle up a rope", my mantra is to *live life in reverse.* Thoreau's "You cannot kill time without injuring eternity" is my life maxim. I herein pledge to sing and write till my finale. Deathbed goal is to say, "I did!" versus "I wish I had." Dear reader, take my "Why not?" oath. *Bon chance.* I humbly submit my offering to your care and grace.

**SUZANNE GRINSLEY WILLIFORD** grew up in Atlanta, GA. She married and moved with her family to San Diego in 1981. She worked for law enforcement and educational agencies. While she wrote often in her professional career, it wasn't until the death of her daughter in 2005 that she decided to write her story for her family and friends. She took a memoir writing class through OSHER Lifelong Learning Institute in 2013 and was a member of the INGLY Writers until her death in 2016.